THE PRAGMATIC INVESTOR™

THE PRAGMATIC INVESTOR™

How To Build Your Wealth In The Stock Market

Mark Hing

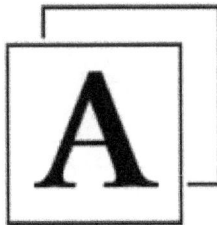

Aptus Communications Inc.

Qualicum Beach, British Columbia

The Pragmatic Investor

First Published 2004

ISBN 978-0-9936441-0-8

Printed in the United States of America

Book cover design by Peter O'Connor (BespokeBookCovers.com)

Published 2014
Published by Aptus Communications Inc. in Canada

DISCLAIMER

This book is sold with the understanding that neither the Author nor the Publisher is engaged in rendering legal, accounting, investing or other professional services by publishing this book. As each individual situation is unique, questions relevant to personal investing and specific to the individual should be addressed to an appropriate professional to ensure that the situation has been evaluated carefully and appropriately.

The Author and Publisher specifically disclaim any liability, loss, or risk which is incurred as a consequence, directly or indirectly, of the use and application of any of the contents of this work.

THE INFORMATION IN THIS BOOK IS PROVIDED "AS IS," AND APTUS COMMUNICATIONS INC. ("APTUS") EXPRESSLY DISCLAIMS ANY IMPLIED OR EXPRESS WARRANTIES OR CONDITIONS OF ANY KIND, INCLUDING WARRANTIES OF MERCHANTABILITY, FITNESS FOR A PARTICULAR PURPOSE, OR NON-INFRINGEMENT OF INTELLECTUAL PROPERTY RELATING TO SUCH MATERIAL. IN NO EVENT SHALL APTUS BE LIABLE FOR ANY DAMAGES WHATSOEVER, INCLUDING (WITHOUT LIMITATION) SPECIAL, INDIRECT, CONSEQUENTIAL OR INCIDENTAL DAMAGES, INCLUDING, WITHOUT LIMITATION, DAMAGES RESULTING FROM USE OF OR RELIANCE ON THE INFORMATION OR SOFTWARE PRESENTED, LOSS OF PROFITS OR REVENUES OR COSTS OF REPLACEMENT GOODS OR LOSS OF GOODWILL.

YOU SHOULD VERIFY ALL CLAIMS AND DO YOUR OWN DUE DILIGENCE BEFORE INVESTING IN ANY SECURITIES MENTIONED.

We encourage you to use caution when investing and educate yourself at the web sites of the Securities and Exchange Commission ("SEC") at www.sec.gov and/or the National Association of Securities Dealers ("NASD") at www.nasd.com. You can review all public filings by companies at the SEC's EDGAR page. The NASD has published information on how to invest carefully at its web site.

CONTENTS

Introduction

"When the map and the territory don't agree, always believe the territory."

Swiss Army Saying

There are two types of people in this world: Those who blaze trails and those who follow a good map. There's no doubt that the thrill of discovery, of finding a path where nobody has tread before or being the first to come up with a new idea is exhilarating, but most of us would be far better off following a map.

As Isaac Newton once said, "If I have been able to see further than others, it is because I have stood on the shoulders of giants." What he meant, of course, was that he had a solid foundation upon which to start. He didn't have to go back and reinvent what others had already done. Rather he could use their efforts as a starting point to further his results.

When it comes to building significant wealth in your lifetime, standing on your own giant's shoulders is not only the most reliable way to go, it's absolutely mandatory. In other words, you must use other people's proven discoveries and learn from their mistakes if you're to be successful. After all, it's good to learn from your mistakes, but it's far better to learn from other people's mistakes.

But back to maps for a moment. A good Map has an interesting attribute. Although it will show you where to go, it won't do the work for you. You still have to arrange the transportation, get the passengers together and actually take the trip. If you don't, although you might know how to get to your desired destination, you'll never get there.

Building wealth is similar. You must have a good, reliable map, but you also need to take action. If you don't then what's the point in reading the map?

This book is your map to building wealth. Once you've read it, and taken the appropriate action, you will significantly improve your chances of successfully building your wealth. In fact it will be very difficult not to be wealthy if you follow its direction.

You'll also minimize the risks that most people take when attempting to build wealth by the seat of their pants.

Think about the last time you tried to find a building somewhere in a new place. Was it easier to look at a map to find your destination or was it easier to set out and simply "discover" that building?

Most people know the correct answer is, "look at the map." Unfortunately, when building wealth, most people choose to blaze their own trails, make mistakes that have been made for hundreds of years and reinvent processes that were known for decades. By the time they discover the correct way to build their wealth, if they ever do, their life is at an end.

They've spent so many years working on the algorithm, that even if they find a good one, they don't have the time to implement it. No wonder there are so many failures.

Success comes to those who have a solid foundation from which to start. The old adage, "you need to crawl before you can walk" contains more than a grain of truth. Without the basics you're relegated to wasting your efforts chasing rainbows rather than concentrating them on moving you closer and closer toward your goal.

Each time you expend any effort it should be with the idea of moving a step further towards your ultimate goal. Any other effort expenditure is wasted.

If you don't know the basics, your chances of succeeding are extremely low. And even with so much media attention given to the stock market, money and investing, the majority of people still won't learn the basics. Why's that?

The reason is that most financial information you receive is noise. Yes it's exciting sometimes, sure it might get the headlines, but in the long run, most of it means nothing.

So if you follow the media reports, if you listen to the so-called "experts," you'll wind up investing in a haphazard manner, you'll have no concrete goals and you won't have anything that even resembles a plan.

If you learn just one thing from this book, it's this, "Think for yourself." Don't be misled by people posing as experts. With some simple basics and your own brain, you can outperform the vast majority of investors, even the professional money managers. No, that's not a misprint. You really can outperform most professional money managers.

This book will show you how to do it. You'll be amazed at how easy it is and how little risk you need to take. Remember, nobody, absolutely nobody cares about your wealth as much as you do.

You're about to begin a journey and you're reading the best map you'll find on the subject of building your wealth. This book will lay out the groundwork for you. It will explain what you need to know in order to implement a solid investment plan.

It assumes that you have a basic knowledge of investment terms and concepts, but if you don't that's okay. Anything that's mentioned (and relevant) but not explained can be easily found on the Internet and understood in less than 10 minutes. Anything that would take you more than 10 minutes to understand is always explained in detail.

Before we begin, here's a quote I like, "Some people make things happen, others watch things happen and others ask, 'Hey, what happened?'"

If you want to build solid wealth you need to position yourself squarely in the first group. It's not difficult and the payoff is so large that I'm constantly amazed at how many people don't even try.

Reinventing the wheel is silly. Not doing your research and jumping blindly into the investment arena is sillier. Finding what worked in the past and what works now is the first step to building your wealth. Sound simple? It is, yet most people don't do it. That's too bad – for them. You, however, are not "most" people. You are a **Pragmatic Investor**. The fact you're reading this means that you're interested in building your wealth in a proven, systematic and efficient manner. And that's exactly what we'll do right now.

So let's get started.

Chapter One
Belief

"If one advances confidently in the direction of his dreams, and endeavors to live the life which he has imagined, he will meet with success unexpected in common hours."

Henry David Thoreau

The overwhelming majority of people today don't believe they can ever be worth millions of dollars. And not surprisingly, they are never worth millions of dollars. That belief ends up costing these investors literally trillions of dollars in lost wealth.

If you have 20 years of time left for your investments to grow, you can definitely become a millionaire. Simply invest $300 a week in an investment averaging 12% annually and in 20 years you'll have more than a million dollars ($1,301,510 to be exact). That's not wishful thinking or gambling, it's a mathematical certainty.

So if you're currently 20 years old, you can have a million dollars by the time you hit 40. That's a time when most of your peers will be grappling with high mortgage payments, child rearing and education costs and, as statistics tell us, large amounts of consumer debt. Yet you'll be a millionaire.

If you're currently 40 and didn't start investing when you were 20, then you're probably not a millionaire. However if you start today, by 60 you will be one. That's a time when most of your peers are struggling to determine whether they can retire comfortably and do all the things they've dreamed of doing after working for many long years. Fortunately you won't be among them, as your retirement will be set.

On the other hand, if you're currently 60 and didn't start investing when you were 40, then you're probably wondering about your retirement future.

However with average first world inhabitants now living well into their 80s, you can still accumulate a million dollars in your life. And this at a time when most of your peers will be wondering how to pay for the increased medical care and supervision they need. You, on the other hand, will have it all taken care of.

Now imagine if you started investing at age 20 and didn't stop until age 70. You'd have $52,255,402 in your account. Even with taxes and inflation that's a lot of money. And it's not a pie-in-the-sky dream, rather it's a mathematical certainty.

So regardless of your stage in life, you can become very wealthy if you simply believe it and then take logical action.

Back in the early 1900s, Albert Einstein gave us more than just new theories about space and time. He also showed us the power of the human mind. Einstein didn't do any experiments to come up with his best known theory, the theory of Relativity, rather he deduced it all in his head.

He demonstrated that pure thought could have a profound effect on reality.

Granted Einstein was a genius when it came to theoretical physics, but he was also human. So if Einstein, without being able to actually see or test it, could come up with a theory that was not obvious and did not appeal to common sense, then the human mind can certainly envision things that are obvious and based on common sense – genius or not.

Investing successfully is not like finding a cure for cancer or discovering the theory of Relativity. It is comparatively much simpler. Too many people make it out to be complicated, but it's not. Just because you haven't done it yet, just because you aren't wealthy yet, doesn't mean that you can't envision how to do it.

Just think, everything you see was once a thought in someone's mind. Buildings, bridges, works of art, inventions and even countries, all began life as a mere thought. That thought grew into a deed which, when it was complete, resulted in a new creation.

Thoughts are real. They're not some abstract, intangible, ethereal phantom that exist only in your mind. Do you think actions determine what you achieve? On the contrary, what you think is what you become because your thoughts control your actions.

Here's an example. I know someone who was severely obese, and not the extra fifty or sixty pounds type of obese either, this guy was more than 300 pounds overweight! Year after year, doctors told him he needed to eat healthier, get some exercise and lose weight. Did he listen? No! Rather than changing his diet he changed his doctors.

Then one day he was diagnosed with a serious problem that was potentially fatal. The choices were either lose weight or stand a good chance of dying. Think about that for a moment. If you were in his shoes what would you do?

If your doctor said that you would die within a year if you didn't exercise for one hour every day and cut out all junk food, would that affect your actions? Would you be up every day exercising and abstaining from junk food? Of course you would. And so did he. The result? He's down to a healthy weight and not facing premature death. And that's the power of thought. When he didn't "think" he was going to die, his actions didn't change. When he "thought" he could die, his actions changed significantly and so did his quality of life.

So it is with your money. What you think directly influences what you have and what you become. If you don't think you can be wealthy, you won't be. But thought alone is not enough.

After all, many people spend a great deal of time thinking about wealth, but they aren't wealthy. The reasons? First, most people dream of being wealthy and think about how they will live when they're worth millions. They don't think about the necessary steps to become wealthy, rather they think about what will happen *when* they're wealthy.

Unfortunately wealth does not just fall into a person's lap. It's something that must be planned. The second reason is that those who think about how they are going to become wealthy either don't have a sound plan or don't take action.

It's not enough to simply think about something, you must believe it with such conviction that it inspires you to take action, overcome all hurdles, and complete what you started. That is the mindset that will make you successful and wealthy. But it all begins with a thought.

Thoughts are powerful indeed. Now what's the thought pattern for most of today's society?

The overwhelming pattern today is that you'll have to work 40-hour weeks until you're 65, and then retire with a "comfortable" income. Not surprisingly, that's what happens with most people.

Of course there's nothing really wrong with that and there are certainly worse things that could happen. However forty or more years of working 40 hours a week only to end up with a "comfortable" income seems a bit harsh to me.

The 40/40 plan is not the only way and it's certainly not the best way.

The secret to obtaining great wealth is to make your money work hard for you, not to make you work hard for your money.

The stark reality is that if most people changed their thinking, by just a little, and started to follow a proven wealth-building plan, they could retire in half the time and be rewarded with a substantial retirement income. That, to me, is a powerful incentive.

Case in point: For many years nobody was able to run a mile in under four minutes. No one "really knew" it could be done.

Then, Roger Bannister did it and lo and behold... dozens of other people did it right after him!

Because now they knew it could be done. I'm telling you right now that you can become wealthy in the stock market. You can't do it overnight, but you *can* do it. It's up to you to believe it with conviction or not.

The ball's in your court.

ACTION PLAN

Think this thought: "I will save one dollar every day."

Then each day take one dollar and put it in a large envelope. That's it! One dollar a day. After a month you'll notice two things. First, your standard of living didn't go down one bit. Second, your envelope will contain about $30. That's 30 extra dollars you normally would not have had. You can spend it on a couple of DVDs or lunch for two at your local bistro, but don't. Keep putting away a dollar a day.

At the end of a year you'll have $365 in that envelope, but the money really doesn't matter. What matters is that you'll have changed your thinking – just a bit. And by doing so you'll have changed your actions which leads to changing your habits which leads to changing your life.

By doing this one little thing, you'll see how powerful a thought can truly be.

Chapter Two

Investment Psychology

"Information is not knowledge."

Albert Einstein

J ust as your thoughts are the basis of what you accomplish, your psychological makeup determines how you perform in the markets. It's important to remember that you have psychological biases. In other words, you have certain preferences and inclinations that inhibit you from objectively evaluating a situation.

Some of these biases are common to all humans while others are specific to you and were created by your personality and life experiences. Regardless of how they came to be, however, you need to understand and control them if you're to be a successful investor.

Now most people like to think they're completely rational and objective when making investment decisions. However research has shown otherwise. To illustrate, consider the following questions: A fair coin is flipped. You receive $200 for heads and nothing for tails or you can refuse to play and collect a guaranteed $100. Which option would you choose? Remember your answer. Now let's change the rules. This time you must pay $200 for heads and nothing for tails or refuse to play and pay $100 immediately. Now which option would you choose?

If you're like most people you'll choose the guaranteed payout in the first case but choose to take a chance in the second case. That's not the behaviour of a rational and objective person. The two games are mirror images of one another so the choices you make should be the same for both – if people were rational and objective that is. However people aren't rational *or* objective, regardless of what they might tell you, so they feel differently about winning and losing. Therefore they make different, irrational, decisions.

This is exactly what Princeton University psychologists, along with Harvard economists, are finding in their latest research. Using an MRI machine to view subjects' brains while they make choices, such as the one described above, professor Jonathan Cohen and Sam McClure are discovering some interesting results.

They've found that humans have two minds: the logical mind and the emotional mind. The logical mind is made up of higher brain functions, which are located in places like the prefrontal cortex, while the emotional mind is more primitive and represented by the limbic system – which is common to all mammals.

According to Cohen, the limbic system harkens back to a time when most things were perishable. If you didn't use it immediately, you lost it. Today, however, that's rarely the case. Food can be preserved in refrigerators or with additives, money can be saved, art can be collected and passed between generations, and the list goes on. We're no longer at a point where we have to use it or lose it. However our limbic system has not changed to take advantage of this new world. We still make many important decisions based on our emotions. We crave instant gratification and short-term action.

While this may have been essential for survival in the primitive world, in today's environment it works against you.

Although economists have long modeled markets by assuming investors and other participants were highly rational; evaluating all options and then always choosing the best one, we know that's not the case in reality. People do not always make rational decisions. In fact, most people make irrational decisions based on emotion rather than logic and facts.

Of course this is nothing new. It was known thousands of years ago and an experiment in 1967 used pigeons to demonstrate exactly that. George Ainslie, at Harvard Medical School, gave the pigeons a choice of being able to immediately get food by pecking a red key or not pecking the key and receiving much more food a short time later. The pigeons all pecked the red key, even when they knew they would receive more food a few seconds later by leaving the key alone.

He then added a green key that, when pecked, stopped the red key from ever appearing. Over time, about a third of the pigeons learned to peck the green key – which gave them more food by forcing them to wait the extra few seconds. Essentially they removed the temptation of immediate gratification from their control because they knew they would be better off by waiting a few seconds to get more food. However, even with this knowledge, they were unable to stop themselves from selecting the red key when they saw it.

Dick Thaler, a noted psychological economist, used Ainslie's work to come to the conclusion that, like the pigeons, successful investors need a mechanism that removes emotion from the investment equation. Unlike the pigeons, however, investors can actually be harmed if they make bad choices, so they need to ensure the mechanism they use really works and is not just an emotional system disguised as a logical one.

Take, for example, the plethora of investment systems that promise overnight riches. These appeal to the limbic system in a big way (by promising to show you how to get rich quickly) and also attempt to appeal to the logical mind (by wrapping an irrational system in a computer software package and thus implying it's a logical way to get rich quickly). Yet upon further analysis, you'll find these systems don't work because computers in and of themselves don't make a bad system good. The old adage, "garbage in, garbage out," definitely applies here.

These, and other, studies clearly show why you, as a **Pragmatic Investor**, need to understand psychology.

The more you know about it the better. You have to understand that certain causes lead to certain emotional reactions, and use that knowledge to increase your returns, minimize your risk and avoid mistakes. Unfortunately understanding psychology is not as simple as most people think.

However it's not all bad news. One of the nice things about psychology is that its principles don't change.

Human nature is the same today as it was ten thousand years ago. It will also be the same ten thousand years from now. In that respect, any effort you expend to learn about human nature today will serve you well into the future.

So what lessons can human nature teach you?

One important lesson is that fear is a powerful motivator. You automatically employ it whenever you feel threatened. Some of the worst investment decisions you make are made largely because of fear.

Buying high and selling low. Staying in low-interest "safe" investments while inflation erodes your capital. Being afraid to do anything. These actions are caused by fear.

All successful investors need to know the basics.

However they also need to be like the Vulcans in Star Trek. The Vulcans had long ago mastered their emotions and disciplined their thoughts. This is the same thing you need to do to be successful in the investment realm. But if you're not a Vulcan and find controlling your emotions difficult or impossible, then you need to "peck the green key" and find a good system that removes your emotions from your investing.

Your emotions cannot play a part in any investment decisions you make. Rather you need to react based on logic, properly filtered information and a sound strategy – no matter what your emotions are presently screaming at you to do.

But this requires you to understand a typical investor's psychology. Your decisions must be made based on the facts, not on what the crowd is doing. If you don't master your emotions, if you don't find a way to overcome them with discipline and logic, you will not be successful. It's as simple as that.

In addition you need to analyze your thought processes to ensure you're not deceiving yourself.

Karen Hochman said, "the greatest obstacle to discovery is not ignorance – it is the illusion of knowledge." Thinking you know something you don't is far worse than not knowing something, but knowing you don't know it.

This illusion of knowledge is caused by many things, but the most prevalent source is the Internet. The Web has dramatically increased the amount of information to which the typical investor has access. Add to that the numerous television shows on investing and you're quickly awash in information.

And while people tend to believe that the more information they have, the better their decisions and the more they know, this is not usually the case. Too much information can cause you to do nothing because you feel overwhelmed. Some information is useless, it's just noise, but the fact you have it tends to make you think you know more, thus the illusion of knowledge.

If you think you know more than you actually do, that tends to breed overconfidence. And overconfident investors generally do poorly in the stock market. They take more risks, they do less research, they rely increasingly on their emotions and they trade more – which increases their trading costs and decreases their returns.

New investors that have a string of good luck right off the bat are more apt to becoming overconfident.

They sometimes mistake pure luck, or a Bull market, for investment skill ("Hey, I think I'll get into this stock market thing." "Gee, I'll buy this stock!"

"It went up!" "It went up again. Say, you want me to teach you how to make loads of money in the stock market…?'").

Keep this in mind: just because you made money it doesn't mean that you're doing the right thing. And if you're not doing the right thing, you will eventually give back all your gains and then some.

If you want to do well, you need to monitor your confidence level. Don't become overconfident in your abilities.

Also related to the illusion of knowledge is the illusion of control. Many investors feel they have control over things that, in reality, they don't.

Some think they can predict the market. Some even think they can control what the market does. It's important to understand what you can actually control and what you can't. Take advantage of the things you can control and position your portfolio so that you have the greatest probability of profiting from the things you can't control.

Speaking of control, one of the things you can definitely control is your thought process. For example, most people have a tendency to place a much higher value on things they own compared to the identical things that they don't own. This is called the Endowment effect and is a flawed way of thinking.

Here's a prime example. My parents were both Realtors. One day they went to list a house and were showing the owner comparable sales in his neighborhood in order to set a reasonable listing price. As it turned out, his house was one of two identical houses built on the same block at the same time by the same builder.

The other house had recently sold for $100,000 less than what he wanted for his. When my parents pointed out the fact that the two houses were identical, he responded by saying that the other house was, "Junk!"

In his mind, his house was worth $100,000 more than the other one because he owned it. He had a psychological attachment to it. However I'm quite sure he would balk at paying $100,000 more for the other one.

As an investor you need to ensure you don't fall into this trap. Simply because you own a stock does not make it more valuable. Every day you should be asking yourself, "if I didn't own this stock but had the equivalent value in cash, would I buy it?" If you can't answer an honest "yes," it might be time to look for another investment.

Remember, always be on the lookout for flawed thinking and when you find yourself thinking this way, take control of your thoughts and bring them back to logical ones.

At first, this can be extremely difficult to do. Many people have spent most of their lives letting their emotions rule their thoughts rather than letting logic do so. So it's no surprise that they aren't in the habit of evaluating situations logically.

As an example, if you already have investments and are faced with too many new options, you'll tend to keep what you have even if there may be a better opportunity in one of the new options. This is called the Status Quo bias.

You should never just accept the status quo. Rather you should objectively and logically analyze all of your options and select the one that gives you the greatest benefit. Sometimes you'll decide to stay with your current investments, even if a more attractive option exists, because switching might be too expensive, too much of an inconvenience or not practical at the time.

However you need to make that decision based on facts, not just by blindly maintaining the status quo.

A related problem is the Attachment bias. This manifests itself when you become attached to your investments. You might have held a stock for years and it might even have appreciated substantially. You could feel some sort of loyalty to it.

So when it stops being a good investment you could have a difficult time selling it.

You might even ignore obvious warning signs or rationalize away some of its problems. This is a manifestation of something psychologists call the Confirmation bias. It's the tendency to hear only what you want to hear and ignore things you don't like. It's related to another bias known as Anchoring, where investors will cling (or anchor themselves) to news that sounds good even if it has no bearing on an objective analysis. They anchor on that news and then seek out information that will support their view while ignoring contradictory information.

Doing any of these things will hurt you financially. Never become married to a stock. If it ceases to be a good investment, sell it.

In addition to these biases, all humans have a primordial need to win and a strong urge to avoid losing. In general this is a healthy trait, however it can work against you when investing.

Most investors tend to hold onto their losers even when the fundamentals change so drastically that it's obvious the stock has turned into a dog. The reason they can't bring themselves to sell it is because that would mean admitting they made a big mistake. As long as they're holding the stock they feel it can come back. Once they sell it, however, they've realized the loss in their minds. And that's painful.

On the flip side, the need to win can cause you to sell a good stock too soon. If your stock appreciates rapidly, but is still a good value at the current price, you might decide to take your profits.

This is never really a bad thing, however if you've done your research and the stock is still a good value, why sell? Unless you have a better use for the proceeds, it makes little sense as it could trigger a tax event, increase your trading costs and cause you to miss out on future appreciation.

But if you do sell, there's another bias waiting for you.

It's called the House-Money effect. When you've just made a profit on an investment, you're more likely to take greater risks when re-investing the proceeds. This is because you feel that you're not investing your money. Rather you're investing free money.

Gamblers who win at the casino call it, "playing with the house's money." This is not a good way to think.

Any profit you make is now **your** money. Treat it as such. It doesn't matter whether you've "owned" the money for 20 years or 20 seconds. It's all your money.

Don't take risks with your new money that you wouldn't be comfortable taking with your old money.

On the flip side there's the Break-Even bias. When your portfolio has lost a significant portion of its value, you tend to take on more risks in an effort to gain back your losses. In essence you try to break even.

However the opposite usually happens and you lose even more because of the additional risks. If your portfolio has already lost money, forget about it. Don't keep a psychological milepost in your head and attempt to reach it at all costs.

You should always be trying to maximize your returns for a given level of risk. Therefore an artificial value that you set based on past events has no advantage.

But it does have a significant disadvantage.

Trying to meet it can cause you to expose yourself to more risk than you'd normally take and increase the probability that you will lose even more.

But let's say you're the rare breed that doesn't suffer from any of these biases. Let's say you've read this far and haven't fallen for anything I've mentioned. Congratulations. But don't pat yourself on the back too quickly.

There is one bias of which almost everyone is guilty. It's called Mental Accounting.

This is the inclination people have to put their money into separate mental accounts. They don't consider the interactions between their financial decisions and thus aren't able to maximize their wealth by using the synergies almost always present in their overall financial picture.

A common situation is when someone has continuing credit card debt and is paying, say, 18% in interest each year. That person might also have a savings account paying him, say, 3% annually. If he used his savings to pay off his credit card he would make an additional 15% a year (after tax!). However because of Mental Accounting, his savings are untouchable, regardless of the fact that using it would significantly maximize his wealth.

Imagine how quickly he'd move his money from his savings account if he found a guaranteed after-tax investment that was paying 18% annually. Well there's one right under his nose, but Mental Accounting obscures it causing him to miss a prime opportunity to increase his wealth with very little effort.

This is something that you should diligently watch for in your financial affairs. Ensure all of your money and assets are working together in the most efficient way possible. Sometimes it's not practical to sell investments to pay off debt, such as when those investments are held in a retirement plan and withdrawing funds would trigger a tax event, but many times there's no logical reason not to and you wind up negatively affecting your financial well-being. Don't practice Mental Accounting, your money does not come with individual labels.

As you can see, there are a number of real psychological biases that can cost you significant amounts of money.

That's why you need a system that removes your emotions and biases from the equation. A system that's been tested and proven to work in many different market scenarios.

With such a system you'll automatically use the best principles, strategies and techniques – even if you don't know you're using them. And if you rely on the system, you'll also automatically remove emotions and psychological biases from your investment decisions.

In essence, you'll make the right choices at times when human nature is telling you to do something else. Something counterproductive. Something that might just be plain silly.

The rest of this book is devoted to showing you how to build a robust, logical system that you can use to avoid these psychological problems.

Now that you've seen a few common biases that can take money right out of your pocket, let's start to look at how we can combat these problems. But first, we need to understand a bit about human nature.

Human nature is such that it tends to out seek things that make us feel good and avoid things that make us feel bad. This is usually a good thing, after all, who in their right mind seeks out bad experiences.

Unfortunately it works against you in the investment arena. The reason is that, in trying to avoid the bad, you tend to minimize the bad things and overemphasize the good things.

This same behaviour can be seen in chronic gamblers. They remember the one time they won a jackpot but forget about the 100 times they lost. So while they remember winning $10,000 they forget they lost $100,000 trying to win in the first place.

But you don't have to visit a casino to see victims. All you need to do is visit your corner store and look at the number of people purchasing lottery tickets.

Although the odds are utterly stacked against a person winning, people nonetheless keep playing.

Why?

It's because a lottery ticket provides what psychologists call *variable reinforcement*. In short, it rewards the player on occasion, but not well enough to logically continue playing (add the fact the big winners are publicized incessantly and you can imagine what every Tom, Dick and Harry are thinking).

However since people like to remember good things and forget bad things, the few rewards that are seen tend to carry greater weight in people's minds than the multitude of times they didn't win. So they keep playing in a futile attempt to hit the jackpot.

In the investment realm the same thing can happen.

Perhaps an investor, acting on a hot tip, buys a very risky penny stock and it does extremely well. Maybe he makes a large profit. Since he likes to remember the good things, he starts to believe that investing in penny stocks using hot tips is the way to go.

In reality, however, that's just a fallacy. It's a bad habit that over the long-term will ensure he loses many more times than he actually wins.

As a Pragmatic Investor, you should never let one positive outcome make you forget all of the negative ones, nor should you use investment plans that are destined to fail because they ensure the odds are stacked against you –

regardless of whether someone you know had a good outcome using such a plan at one time.

Common sense will tell you that this is not the way to build your wealth.

In essence, you should not make decisions based on an outcome, but on a proven process. If your friend recently won 5 million dollars in the lottery (beating the 14 million-to-one odds), that outcome doesn't mean that your best retirement strategy is to purchase lottery tickets – because the probability is that you won't be able to repeat your friend's feat.

On the other hand, if your uncle made 5 million dollars following a sound, proven long-term investment strategy over the past 30 years, it would be well worth your while to copy the process he used, because in 30 years the probability is you'd see similar results. That's the difference between basing decisions on an outcome versus a proven process.

Of course even if you're following a sound plan you can still lose (because of bad luck or some such thing), but don't let it get you down. Continue following your plan; over the long-term a proven plan typically pays off.

A good plan increases your chances of seeing a favorable outcome, but it doesn't guarantee it. Bad things happen. That's a fact.

And you can't change that fact by pretending it doesn't matter. You can't change it by sticking your head in the sand and going to your happy place and you certainly can't change it by forgetting it happened.

That line of thinking sets you up for failure in so many ways. If something goes wrong, see if you can learn something from it. See if you can use that information to tweak your plan.

Former Tennis star John McEnroe said, "the important thing is to learn a lesson every time you lose." And that sums it up nicely. You will lose sometimes. Get used to it. The important thing is to learn from that loss and then do something about it so that you don't make the same mistake, that caused your loss, again in the future.

If you don't do this you're bound to continue making the same mistakes forever. So what are some common mistakes that people make over and over again?

Consider these questions. Do you believe the general market cares about you? Can you influence the market? Do you think it's okay to follow hot stock tips without doing your own due diligence? Is the market different this time? Do you think you can predict the market? Do you get angry when the market moves against you? Have you ever given into greed when things are going well? Do you take full responsibility for your gains but blame something "out of your control" when you lose? Are you ignoring risk and just focusing on returns?

If you answered "Yes" to any of these questions, then you've made a common investment mistake.

Here's a fact: you can't affect the market anymore than you can affect a tornado. However, like a tornado, the market can definitely affect you. And if you don't have a sound plan, it can devastate your portfolio and the plans and dreams built on that portfolio.

If you want to be a successful investor over the long term, you need to be aware of your true limitations. You need to be practical, logical and have a plan in place *before* you enter the market.

You also need to keep your ego in check and realize that you are one very small, miniscule, tiny cog in a vast machine that, like a force of nature, will continue to move along its merry way no matter what you do or don't do.

The best that you can hope for is to ride its coattails and *react* to its movements in a manner that is favorable to you.

That's what we'll discuss in the remainder of the book, but before we delve into specific strategies, it's useful to take a moment and look at the best of the best.

And when it comes to investing, nobody has done it better over the past five decades than Warren Buffet.

ACTION PLAN

Reread this chapter and ensure that you aren't guilty of any of the psychological biases mentioned.

If you find one that describes you, think about how to change it. That might mean automating a process to take the decision out of your hands, or it might mean something else.

Do whatever it takes to rid yourself of these biases.

The sooner you do, the faster you'll be able to build your wealth.

Chapter Three
Warren Buffett

"There seems to be some perverse human characteristic
that likes to make easy things difficult."

Warren Buffett

B uffett grew up in Omaha, Nebraska and at an early age had a knack
for numbers. He could keep track of complex calculations in his
head and liked to think things through in a logical manner.

So it came as no surprise that he took an immediate liking to Benjamin
Graham's classic book, "The Intelligent Investor," when he first read it in
University. The premise of value investing, with its focus on numbers and
logic, appealed to the young Buffett on a number of different levels.

He was so drawn to the ideas in the book that he left Omaha to study
under Graham in New York, eventually going to work for him in 1954.

After his stint with Graham, at the ripe old age of 25, Buffett returned to
Omaha and started his, now fabled, limited investment partnership. He ran it
mainly using the value techniques he learned from his mentor Graham. It
succeeded spectacularly, exceeding even Buffett's own expectations.

Over a thirteen-year period, Buffett's annual compounded returns were
29.5% and he never had a losing year.

Today, Buffett is still going strong. His annual Berkshire Hathaway reports
are as entertaining as they are informative and provide a unique insight into
the mind of the man they call the Oracle of Omaha.

Some of those insights can teach us how to invest like Warren Buffett
while others are interesting to read, but not very useful in a practical sense
because they are either unique to Buffett or depend upon his vast resources to
which the average investor does not have access.

Even so, there is enough pragmatic wisdom in Buffett's teachings to keep
the Oracle's acolytes reading and learning for many long years.

When it comes to investing, there are three basic things that you must possess and master if you're to be successful. They are, in order, Control of your Emotions, Knowledge and the ability to apply that Knowledge.

On the emotional front, Buffett learned from, who else but, Benjamin Graham.

Graham considered a stock's price to be made up of two parts: an underlying intrinsic value part and a speculative component. The underlying value could be determined using accurate numbers and logic. The speculative component (which could be positive or negative) depended mainly on human emotions, such as fear and greed, and could not be calculated in advance.

Knowing this, Buffett was able to constantly exploit investors who invested illogically because of their emotions.

He used Graham's euphemism of Mr. Market to describe how sometimes Mr. Market offers to purchase your stocks at very high prices because he's in a cheery mood. Everything looks good to him and he's highly optimistic about the future.

At other times Mr. Market is downright gloomy. He thinks the bottom is about to fall out of the economy and just wants to get rid of his stocks. Thus he offers them to you at very low prices.

The main thing to remember is that the actual stock's intrinsic value hasn't changed; the only thing that's changed is Mr. Market's emotions and thus his mood.

At any given time you can sell your shares to Mr. Market, buy his shares or simply ignore his offers and repeat the entire process the next day.

What Graham is saying, in effect, is that when someone acts stupidly because of his emotions, dive in and exploit the situation. Sounds harsh right? That's because it is harsh. Unfortunately that's the world of investing.

If you want to become really wealthy, you have to take advantage of people with less knowledge or those who don't control their emotions well.

When you unload your overpriced stock, another human being is on the other end buying it. When that stock plummets, that human being loses money, perhaps lots of money. Perhaps even his house and other assets. That's not what most people think about when they trade stocks, but it is the reality. The trick is to ensure that you aren't the person buying overpriced stocks and losing money.

Exploiting other people's emotions is one thing, but keeping a lid on your own emotions is quite another matter altogether. Yet Buffett excels here too. He knows how to effectively deal with his emotions.

That's not to say that he's a Vulcan. He's still human. And rest assured he has the same urges and emotional needs all humans do, but his strength is in how he deals with those urges and needs.

Most people aren't disciplined enough to always do the right thing when their emotions are running high.

That's why they need a mechanical system to execute their investment plans for them. That way, emotions are kept out and logic is preserved.

Unfortunately the majority of investors don't use such systems. They continue to rely on their emotions, losing money and exposing themselves to much more risk than they need to.

To Buffett, emotions are like a double-edged sword. They can hurt you if you let them or they can enrich you if you view them as an opportunity to profit from others who don't keep such a tight handle on theirs.

He loves the fact that he can buy great companies at huge discounts because others are blinded by fear.

And he regularly quotes Benjamin Graham's quintessential line, "you are neither right or wrong because the crowd disagrees with you. You are right because your data and reasoning are right."

That's classic Buffett, breaking the market down into numbers and logic. And that's one of the key elements to his success: keeping his emotions out of his investing decisions.

In the next chapter we'll take a closer look at emotions and see why they can end up costing you a bundle.

ACTION PLAN

Visit Warren Buffett's Berkshire Hathaway Web site at www.BerkshireHathaway.com and read through some of Buffett's letters to Berkshire shareholders.

The site itself is not much to look at, but the information it contains is invaluable to investors.

It's like taking a top-notch course in practical investment methods. And it's available to you at no charge – whether you're a Berkshire shareholder or not.

Chapter Four

Emotions

"If you are shopping for common stocks, choose them the way you would buy groceries, not the way you would buy perfume."

Benjamin Graham

Your emotions can derail even the best laid investment plans. In order to succeed, you must eliminate emotion from your decisions. If you succumb to fear, greed or the multitude of other negative emotions, your investments will suffer.

However overcoming your emotions is easier said than done. That's why it's crucial to select a proven investment system and stick with it. When in doubt, trust your system, not your emotions.

There's an old Wall Street adage that sums this thought up nicely, "Bulls make money, Bears make money, but Pigs get slaughtered."

The funny thing is most people don't learn from it. When markets are going great guns, many investors turn into speculators as a wave of greed engulfs and then blinds them to the dangers of purchasing high-risk equities.

In a fit of unthinking greed, normally conservative, clear-thinking individuals roll the dice, with their life savings on the line, hoping to hit the jackpot. As the hype builds, more and more sane people turn into lemmings following hot tips and high-profile analysts' recommendations. All without doing their homework, performing their own due diligence or using their inbred common sense.

As you might imagine, this is a recipe for disaster because the markets usually turn quickly and without mercy. Having been caught once, some investors, now engulfed in fear, turn into chickens and vow never again to enter the stock market. Unfortunately this too is a recipe for disaster because although chickens don't lose money, they don't make much either.

So what do we have so far? Bulls, Bears, Pigs, Lemmings and Chickens. These beasts make up the zoo we all know as the stock market. Now if you ask most people, they'll undoubtedly say they're either Bulls or Bears. Some honest ones might say they're Chickens, but I don't think many would call themselves Lemmings or Pigs.

But just as 80% of drivers believe their driving skills are in the top half of all drivers (think about that for a second), most investors aren't Bulls or Bears. Rather they start off as Lemmings and quickly become Pigs before flying into full Chicken mode.

The trick is to honestly evaluate yourself. If you're not a Bull or a Bear, create a plan for becoming one. You might even want to be a Bull sometimes and a Bear at other times, and that's okay – as long as you don't become one of the other animals.

Don't fall into the trap of blindly following the lemmings. When you find a situation that you understand and have facts to back you up, take immediate action and ignore advice from the pigs, lemmings and chickens. There's also another animal in the zoo, that you'd do well to ignore too, but I'll get to it later. For now let's look at why stock prices fluctuate.

Any high school economics student can tell you that prices fluctuate because of supply and demand. As demand (when there are more buyers than sellers) for a stock increases, its price will increase. When supply (there are more sellers than buyers) increases, its price will decrease. The equilibrium price will be at the point where demand equals supply. The question then becomes, "What causes demand and supply to change?"

In a logical world where information is available to everyone at the same time, stock prices would be based on a company's actual and potential earnings in addition to its assets.

Good companies will be worth more in the future because they earn profits and retain some (or all) of those profits. This increases the value of the company and thus its stock price rises to reflect this.

Equilibrium would then be established at that price.

For example, let's look at the concession stand at the zoo. If it's owned by 10 people (i.e. has 10 shares outstanding), has $100 in assets (it's a small zoo) and makes a profit of $10 a day, then each share would be worth $10 today. Tomorrow, however, the concession would be worth $110 and each share would be worth $11. The day after that each share would be worth $12. Following this line of reasoning you can see how the value of the concession stand grows over time. It's also possible that a Bull would be willing to pay $11 for a share today with the expectation of selling it two days from now for $12.

However only a lemming or a pig would be willing to pay $100 a share. The lemming would pay because he's following others without thinking for himself and the pig would pay because he's hoping to find a greedier pig that will pay him $110 tomorrow.

Similarly if a company is positioned to grow its earnings at a relatively higher rate in the future, investors should be willing to pay more for its stock and equilibrium would be established at the higher price. So if our concession stand makes $200 a day in profit, rather than just $10 a day, investors should be willing to pay relatively more today with the expectation of being rewarded with a relatively more valuable company tomorrow.

Unfortunately the world is not logical and that's where the problems begin. Stock prices are not based solely on facts and numbers. There's also an enormous emotional component.

That's why many Internet companies were worth hundreds of millions during the dotcom heyday although they had few assets, no earnings and no hope of ever making a profit.

Underlying value had nothing to do with their valuation; rather it was based on wild speculation, unchecked emotion, overzealous optimism, hype and greed. In other words, the lemmings and pigs were running around the zoo telling everyone they were Bulls (the real Bulls found it quite amusing and the Bears made out like bandits).

And another animal, the Weasel, was laughing all the way to the bank (fortunately the average investor can't become a Weasel, that's the exclusive domain of analysts, investment bankers and, sometimes, senior company executives).

Recall that you don't want to be a lemming, a chicken or a pig. So what can you do?

If you want to do well in the stock market you must think for yourself. That bears repeating, THINK FOR YOURSELF. And you can start by realizing that the major reason stock prices fluctuate, in the short-term, is because of psychological reasons rather than valuation ones.

It's actually quite amazing how many people think stock prices are based solely on facts and that all of the facts are reflected in the price. That's not how the markets operate. While based loosely on facts, they're based mostly on how people feel.

And anytime you bring in people's feelings, you're dealing with emotions, usually devoid of facts, and therefore you can't reliably predict what they will be thinking. In other words you cannot consistently predict price movements over the short-term. Period. No matter what the weasels, lemming and pigs would have you believe.

But don't just take my word for it. John Graham at the University of Utah and Campbell Harvey at Duke University analyzed over 15,000 predictions from 237 market timing newsletters from 1980 to 1992 and concluded that, "there is no evidence that newsletters can time the market." In fact, by the end of the study over 94% of the newsletters had gone out of business.

It seems that not only did they do a poor job of predicting the market, but they also did a poor job of predicting their business success!

Further evidence against short-term prediction comes from Mark Hulbert, who runs a very popular newsletter rating service. Hulbert studied 25 market-timing newsletters from 1988 to 1997 and found that none, not one, beat the S&P 500 index. In fact the average return over the period was just 11.06% compared to the S&P 500's 18.06%.

Now if this all sounds like a hopeless situation, take heart because there is good news. You can do reasonably well predicting the market over the long-term (it tends to go up), that's why the Buy and Hold strategy works.

You can also take advantage of short-term price fluctuations after the fact by buying on dips and selling into rallies (implemented through portfolio rebalancing, see Chapter Thirteen for details).

The key to this reactive approach is that you take action AFTER the fact and thus eliminate the need to predict anything in the short-term.

Unfortunately no one strategy is perfect and that's why it's a good idea to not only diversify your assets, but also diversify your investment strategies. Some strategies will work better than others at different times and in different markets. So diversifying will ensure you don't have all of your investment eggs relying on one strategy.

The five major rules to remember are:

1. Think for yourself.
2. Don't follow any strategy that requires you to predict short-term stock price moves.
3. Be a Bull and/or a Bear, but never be a chicken, a lemming or a pig.
4. Don't listen to the weasels unless you can verify what they say with proper, conclusive facts.
5. Diversify your assets as well as your investment strategies.

If you do nothing else but adhere to these rules, you should come out significantly ahead of the majority of investors who're blindly chasing the next hot thing but never making any real profits in order to efficiently build their wealth.

Remember, it's human nature to be emotional and to act on emotion. And two of the most powerful emotions are greed and fear.

When others around you are making large sums of money by buying the latest hot stocks, greed will tell you that, "you're missing out."

Without realizing it you're in with the masses purchasing stocks you know nothing about. When the bottom falls out, fear kicks in, you panic and sell with the crowd. In other words you buy high and sell low. Common sense will tell you that's not how you make money in the stock market.

I think Warren Buffett summed it up nicely when he said, "the financial calculus that [we] employ would never permit our trading a good night's sleep for a shot at a few extra percentage points of return. I've never believed in risking what my family and friends have and need in order to pursue what they don't have and don't need."

That's sound advice indeed.

ACTION PLAN

Start by evaluating your current portfolio and the reasons why you purchased the stocks you did. Write them down. If you don't have a good reason for owning a stock (and "my best friend says it will go through the roof" is not a good reason) then think about getting out of that stock and purchasing something that you do have a good reason to buy.

Chapter Five

Wealth

"The real measure of your wealth is how much you'd be worth
if you lost all your money."

Anon.

I don't remember the first time I saw the movie, "Casablanca," in one sitting, but I do recall seeing most of the film in parts. If it was on TV I would watch a bit, usually because everyone kept saying how good it was, then start thinking that, "this film is in black and white, there's no action or special effects and parts of it are quite corny," and then I'd turn it off.

I did this for years, each time happening to watch another part before eventually turning it off. Before I knew it I had actually seen the entire film, albeit out of order, but I still had no idea what it was about. And I still believed the common fallacy that Rick had actually said, "Play it again Sam."

Then one day I decided to sit through the entire show. What a surprise! It immediately became one of my favorite films of all time. The story, the acting and, yes, even the corn fit together beautifully. I subsequently discovered that Rick had not actually said, "Play it again Sam," but "If she can stand it, I can. Play it!" Needless to say, I've continued to watch it over and over again.

Now you might be wondering what all this has to do with investing and building wealth, but rest assured the parallels are startling. I first twigged on the unlikely fact that Casablanca could teach me how to build wealth when I remembered how long it had taken me to actually sit down and watch the entire film. I had been doing the same thing with my money.

From time to time I'd read or hear something about building investments, net worth and wealth. I'd think about it for awhile, usually because the experts kept saying that was the thing to do, and then proceed to tune it out and turn it off. Eventually I had heard everything I needed to succeed in my wealth building endeavors, albeit out of order, but I had no idea how to go about it.

And I believed the common fallacy that I couldn't amass enough wealth to make a real difference in my life.

It wasn't until I sat down and "saw the whole picture" that the light bulb went on. It was then I started to notice the little lessons in Casablanca and soon discovered the spirit of those lessons could be applied directly to building wealth. I realized it was quite simple to accumulate a small fortune based on this information. Not easy, mind you, but simple. To succeed requires patience, discipline and a strong desire to accomplish the feat, but it is definitely worth it.

If you're stuck in a 9 to 5 world just waiting for the whistle to blow so you can begin your retirement after having worked your entire adult life, there is a better way. You can become financially independent by simply changing your thinking, your expectations and your financial practices. After all, the best things in life are free, but money buys you the time to enjoy them.

In the film, Victor Laszlo believed he could help defeat the Nazis. Even when he was in a German concentration camp that belief helped him keep the resistance's secrets. At Rick's Café, when Major Strasser offered Laszlo a pair of exit visas in exchange for the names of the underground resistance leaders, Laszlo responded by saying, "if I didn't give them to you in a concentration camp, where you had more persuasive methods at your disposal, I certainly won't give them to you now."

Laszlo's unwavering belief that the resistance would eventually triumph gave him the strength to take the hard road and overcome the seemingly insurmountable obstacles the Third Reich was continually putting in front of him. He sacrificed a great deal, but never lost his belief he would one-day reach his goal.

Without that belief, he would have been just another man captured or killed by the invading Germans. Instead he became a hero, a beacon to others and a leader of men. His goal was simple: to get out of Casablanca so he could help the resistance. It wasn't an easy goal, but it was a simple one. The main thing to note is he had a goal. He didn't simply blunder around Casablanca chasing rainbows. Everything he did, from attending the secret resistance meeting to obtaining exit visas, was done to bring him one step closer to his goal.

Laszlo had decided early on he was going to do something about his situation. He developed a plan, implemented it, sacrificed and then persevered to bring about the desired results.

If you want to build wealth, your thoughts need to be like Victor Laszlo's. There will undoubtedly be many obstacles along the way and you'd do well to emulate his unwavering conviction.

Fortunately, as you're building your wealth, you won't have to sacrifice nearly as much as Laszlo did. However you will have to implement a plan, persevere and see it through to completion.

It goes without saying, then, that in order to build wealth, you need to know what wealth is. The dictionary defines wealth to be abundance, affluence, and riches. That's a fair definition, but it is somewhat vague. For example, some might say that high-income earners are wealthy, others that people with an excess of material goods are wealthy. While these definitions capture some aspect of wealth, they ultimately miss the mark.

I define wealth to be, "the amount of time you have for yourself and the resources to do what you want with that time." Time is the most valuable asset you have. Simply put, if you can't use your time as you like, then you aren't wealthy. If you can, then you are.

In the film, a German banker tried to cash a Deutschebank check (considered Nazi, or dirty, money) and was taken aback when Rick refused to let him cash it. "Your cash is good at the bar," Rick had said just before tearing up the check. "What? Do you know who I am?" the banker replied. "I do, you're lucky the bar's open to you," was Rick's response before walking away.

That German banker had money in the form of a check, but he was in a situation where he couldn't use it. Similarly if someone has billions of dollars in the bank, but can't use it because he's forced to work 20 hours a day, then that person is not really wealthy.

This is not usually obvious to most people.

Of course someone worth billions can pay others to perform tasks and thus free up time. So while it's easier to become truly wealthy if you have an abundance of money, the point is that if you really can't enjoy your billions the way you want, you're not wealthy.

If, on the other hand, you have very little money then you're not wealthy either. This is glaringly obvious to almost everyone. No money directly translates into no wealth. The newly married Bulgarian couple, Jan and Annina, fit this category. They had traveled from Bulgaria to escape the dictator Tsar Boris III's reign of terror. Unfortunately their travels had been more difficult and expensive than they had thought, so when they reached Casablanca they didn't have enough money to obtain exit visas.

Jan was at the roulette wheel trying to win the needed money, but he was losing the little money they had left. So Annina asked Rick for advice on whether to accept the visas, from police chief Louis Renault, in exchange for sleeping with the womanizing captain. Rick's advice? "Go back to Bulgaria."

Annina was so concerned about solving a short-term problem that she was willing to morally bankrupt herself to achieve it. She wasn't looking at the long-term future she was to have with Jan. What would happen when the couple arrived in America with no money? Would she decide to sleep with the grocer to put food on the table? What would happen when Jan found out?

Her thoughts were in stark contrast to Victor Laszlo's, who always had his eye on the long-term goal and was unwilling to compromise his principles in order to solve a short-term problem.

Unlike Annina, Laszlo didn't focus on his immediate situation, which at times seemed hopeless. Had he done so, he might have been tempted to make a deal with the Nazis and give them the names of other rebel leaders in exchange of his and Ilsa's freedom.

Instead he took a long-term view and realized that his real goal wasn't to escape from Casablanca, but it was to defeat the Nazis. Escaping Casablanca was a short-term goal that moved him one step closer to accomplishing the real goal. It would not be prudent to sacrifice his long-term objective, the true goal, merely to accomplish a short-term one. So when Major Strasser suggested he provide the resistance leaders' names, Laszlo declined.

If you want to build wealth, it's a good idea to follow Victor Laszlo's example, not Annina's. Building wealth Annina's way means doing anything to get what you want, compromising principles and sacrificing the true, long-term, goal to solve a short-term problem. Since the true goal is the main point, losing it because of a short-term problem is sheer lunacy.

But back to Jan and Annina. They had a great deal of time, but no money to do what they wanted with their time – in this case, start a family in America. Similarly if someone chooses not to work and therefore has a great deal of time, but no money to use the time according to his or her wishes, then he or she is not wealthy either.

It bears repeating that to be truly wealthy, you must have the time and resources to do what you want, when you want. To some that means traveling extensively, others want a big house and fancy cars, and still others are happy to simply entertain family and friends whenever they want to.

True wealth is an individual thing that is different for different people. The only constant is that wealth is a tool that people use to give them the free time and resources to pursue what they want to do in life, not what others want them to do. And you can learn how to go about correctly amassing your fortune from an old black and white film.

"Louis, I think this is the beginning of a beautiful friendship." But that's not the end of the story.

There's another reason people don't build wealth successfully. And like most pitfalls it's based on ego, emotion and human nature.

To illustrate, let's go back to the 1980s when Miami Vice was the hottest show on television and Don Johnson had just scored a new Ferrari Testarossa.

When I first saw it on TV, I decided then and there that that was the car for me!

Unfortunately Testarossas were going for about $250,000 at the time. After adding up my savings, I found I was $248,000 short – not to mention the cost of taxes and insurance. Needless to say, I didn't get the Ferrari.

Then a few years ago my wife and I found ourselves in the unenviable position of looking for a new (to us anyway) vehicle. After doing some research, I created a short list for consideration. There were two trains of thought running through my mind when I created the list.

The first was to get a nice practical vehicle.

The other was to sell the house, cash in the savings, and plunk it all down on a brand new Ferrari. Of course I understood that we could buy eight very nice vehicles for the cost of one Ferrari. But the Ferrari has a top speed of 181 mph and can accelerate from 0 to 60 in 5.4 seconds! That means I can (theoretically) make the trip from my house to my office in downtown Vancouver, 30 miles away, in less than 10 minutes. And merging onto the freeway? Absolutely no problem whatsoever. I wondered what my wife would say (actually I knew what she would say, but sometimes you have to ask to be sure).

"We are not selling our house to buy a Ferrari!" And with those words my hopes of owning a fine Italian driving machine were dashed for a second time. So we settled on a two year old Toyota Camry.

Now there's nothing wrong with a Camry. Compared to a Ferrari it gets better gas mileage and is cheaper to insure, maintain, and repair. It also has more room for passengers and baggage. Furthermore the traffic from my house to the office generally moves at 30 mph during the morning commute – so the Camry's top speed is more than adequate. And we can purchase it outright and don't have to sell the house.

So from a logical, common sense, point of view, I think we can all agree the Camry is the better choice. If you were in my shoes, you'd probably nix the Ferrari idea too. Given this, you might wonder why the Ferrari is so appealing? I can only assume it is for one reason and one reason only: Flash (or head-turning ability). Nobody stops to look as a Toyota drives by. Neither does anyone pull up beside a Camry, roll down the window, and say "Niiiiiiiice car!" And I've yet to see a case where someone, on the sidewalk, will turn to a Camry driver and give him a hearty "thumbs up." Rather, the Toyota is pretty much invisible. Just another vehicle on the street.

Even with the Ferrari's head-turning ability, however, it's easy to see that purchasing the Camry is the better idea. Unfortunately I believe that many of us make Ferrari decisions without consciously realizing it. Case in point, how many times has someone you know borrowed money to buy a brand new luxury car? How about financing a vacation using a credit card? Or buying stereos and furniture on the "don't pay until the New Year" plan and then not being able to pay when the New Year arrives? And the list goes on.

One of the biggest problems in Western Civilization today is people don't realize they can't afford half the things they buy.

In saner times people believed they could afford something if they had the *cash* in the bank to purchase it outright. Today, people think they can afford something if they can make the minimum payments.

Are we so mathematically challenged we can't extrapolate where this kind of thinking will lead us?

The mentality seems to be it's our "right" to own a big house, new cars and the latest consumer goods. And the credit card companies are right there confirming it. Unfortunately this type of thinking is upside down.

Now there's nothing wrong with owning life's luxuries, but only if you go about it the right way. Which of courses brings up the question of, "what is the right way?"

The upside down approach is to purchase luxury items before having the proper resources to do so.

There are a surprising number of high-income earners that aren't wealthy. In fact these people are carrying so much debt, the average welfare recipient is better off.

These are the people who will quietly laugh to themselves and think, "that man can't afford to buy this $5 cappuccino because he's on social assistance. I am so fortunate to have my high paying job." Then they'll nonchalantly charge the cappuccino to their nearly maxed out credit card. Of course they won't pay it off at the end of the month and thus will incur an absurdly high interest charge. All the while they'll continue to go through life oblivious to the fact they are really only a few paycheques away from bankruptcy. Truly the wealth-challenged live in a fantasy world all their own.

The correct approach is to live within (or even below) your means and concentrate on building your wealth.

This leads to cash flow generation, which then leads to the ability to purchase expensive consumer goods without incurring debt.

The wealth-challenged skip right to the part where they purchase the expensive consumer goods, because they want instant gratification and, perhaps, others to look at them with more than just a little envy. In essence they go for the Flash. They then spend the next few years working hard to pay for their purchases. In fact the cycle of debt usually continues and they inevitably spend their entire lives building wealth for others (such as the banks) rather than themselves.

Add to that the wealth-challenged person's usual habit of spending more whenever he or she receives a raise, bonus or unexpected windfall, and you can see why obtaining wealth becomes an impossible dream. It never occurs to the wealth-challenged to stop spending, pay off debts and invest. Rather this person has been hypnotized into believing a myth of epic proportions: that "wants" are actually "needs." A sad state of affairs at the best of times, but a potentially deadly one for someone with mounting debts.

What's more, you don't have to be severely wealth-challenged to buy into the myth. Many "regular folks" unwittingly mortgage their future to obtain a few "must have" consumer items "right now." Although they may not be anywhere near bankruptcy, they will never be truly wealthy either.

There are many ways to build wealth, but it comes down to doing two main things.

First, stop spending and concentrate on eliminating all debt (especially high-interest consumer debt) as soon as possible. By doing so you're able to keep more of your earned income for yourself. In other words, if you're in a hole, stop digging.

Most people shouldn't be investing in anything (other than perhaps the house in which they live) until they've paid off their credit cards and other consumer debts. By eliminating debt (that isn't backed by an increasing asset), you earn a guaranteed after-tax rate of return equal to the interest you're currently paying.

So if your credit card interest is 18% a year, you'll earn 18% (after-tax!) annually by simply paying it off.

Where else are you going to find those returns?

Second, convert earned income into growth and income producing assets as quickly as possible. These assets can take various forms, but the most common are stocks, bonds and mutual funds. Such assets increase in value over time without the need for their owners to actively work for the gains.

People who have no debts and whose wealth increases every year, without them actively working for it, are in the best position to purchase luxury items. Their money works for them 24 hours a day, every day of the year – even when they're vacationing on the French Riviera. And these are the people most able to purchase, say, a Ferrari from the proceeds of their growing assets.

Most people don't believe they can do it at first, but nevertheless it is a realizable goal – especially if you start young. Everyone's goal should be to generate enough income from their investments, so they can more than comfortably live without the need to actively work.

Hopefully you're well on your way to eliminating your debts and building your wealth through sound investments.

So the next time you're thinking of borrowing money to vacation in the Bahamas (the Ferrari decision), give your head a shake and settle for the Bed and Breakfast around the corner (the Toyota decision).

It may not elicit envious stares from your friends, but you'll sleep better knowing you're right side up, building your wealth so that one day you'll not only vacation in the Bahamas, but you just might purchase a winter residence there. Mortgage free.

Now that you know what wealth is and, more importantly, how to go about building it, let's drill down and look at the details.

Simply by knowing the definition of wealth (remember it's not just how much money you have or how much you make each year), you're further along than most people. But it's not enough. You need to concentrate your efforts on building your wealth in the most efficient manner possible.

If you don't, you'll waste time. And time is the one thing you cannot retrieve. Once it's gone, it's gone. And gone with it is the opportunity to use compounding over time to automatically build your wealth.

So how can you build wealth efficiently? The answer lies in a Thomas Kinkade painting.

That painting depicts a rapid stream running by tranquil shores. The stream turns a wooden wheel and the wheel runs a mill. Sounds nice doesn't it?

Unfortunately, most of the stream's potential is wasted.

If someone knew about generators and turbines and took the time to install some in the appropriate place, that same stream could produce enough electricity to run many mills.

Think about that stream when you see all the so-called "expert" information being lapped up by today's investors. That information is everywhere, television, newspapers, magazines, the Internet and that's just the beginning.

All of that wealth-building potential is being wasted.

If investors would cut through the garbage, filter the noise and follow a proven plan, they'd be able to create enormous wealth for themselves and their children. They'd be running a multitude of mills instead of barely turning the waterwheel to run one small one.

But you don't have to be a one-mill investor. You don't have to rely on marketing hype, get-rich-quick stocks or luck. Rather you can rely on proven methods that have been successful for many decades.

You can rely on hard facts, tested systems and techniques that have already made others very wealthy. And in the end you'll be richly rewarded while almost everyone else continues to chase the elusive pot of gold by flitting from one unproven system to another, year after year, in a vain attempt to get rich quickly.

It's sad really. Naïve investors paying high mutual fund fees to money managers who can't even beat the indexes.

In fact 80% of actively managed mutual funds under-perform their associated indexes. This leaves investors with far less than they should have. Rather than the investors retiring rich, the fund managers are the ones who retire with the lion's share of the money.

The stock market is fraught with wasted effort, indecision, fear, greed and deceit. Investment newsletters promising the world for only $300 a year but falling far short of the mark.

And it's not just the new investors that are taken, many who have been in the market for a very long time have no idea how to invest properly (there's a big difference between being an investor with 20 years' experience and being an investor with no experience who's been in the market for 20 years).

The investment industry is growing every year, but individual investors aren't benefiting as they should. Most investors don't know the risks to which they're exposing themselves. Most don't know how to read even the most rudimentary financial statements nor do they know how to analyze a company's fundamentals.

Think about that. Billions of dollars are being invested in the market without the knowledge of basic fundamentals or knowing the risks involved.

That's as certain a recipe for disaster as I've seen.

The bottom line is that building wealth in the stock market is not exciting. In fact it's simple and boring.

Building wealth the correct way might not seem attractive to you if you're looking for cocktail party chatter. But building wealth over time is the only way to become rich without taking unnecessary risks.

So how are you doing? Thomas Stanley and William Danko, in their book, "The Millionaire Next Door," give a rough formula for computing what your wealth should be right now. Here's an excerpt.

"Multiply your age times your realized pretax annual household income from all sources except inheritances. Divide by ten. This, less any inherited wealth, is what your net worth should be.

For example, if Mr. Anthony O. Duncan is forty-one years old, makes $143,000 a year, and has investments that return another $12,000, he would multiply $155,000 by forty-one. That equals $6,355,000. Dividing by ten, his net worth should be $635,500. If Ms. Lucy R. Frankel is sixty-one and has a total annual realized income of $235,000, her net worth should be $1,433,500.

Given your age and income, how does your net worth match up? Where do you stand along the wealth continuum? If you are in the top quartile for wealth accumulation, you are a PAW, or prodigious accumulator of wealth. If you are in the bottom quartile, you are a UAW, or under accumulator of wealth. Are you a PAW, a UAW, or just an AAW (average accumulator of wealth)?

We have developed another simple rule. To be well positioned in the PAW category, you should be worth twice the level of wealth expected. In other words, Mr. Duncan's net worth/wealth should be approximately twice the expected value or more for his income/age cohort, or $635,500 multiplied by two equals $1,271,000. If Mr. Duncan's net worth is approximately $1.27 million or more, he is a prodigious accumulator of wealth. Conversely, what if his level of wealth is one-half or less than expected for all those in his income/age category? Mr. Duncan would be classified as a UAW if his level of wealth were $317,750 or less (or one-half of $635,500)."

How do you stack up? Don't worry if you're not a PAW just yet. By finishing this book and taking the appropriate action you'll be well on your way. After all, just as Rome wasn't built in a day, so too your wealth takes time to accumulate.

Building wealth is a long-term pursuit. So be patient.

Don't be like the majority of people who base their actions on the short-term view. Actions such as going into debt to finance consumer goods, taking out a larger mortgage than they can reasonably afford and lengthening the amortization period or working at a dead end job simply because it pays more than a job where they could gain knowledge that would benefit them in the long run.

Let's look at an example.

Suppose you had just completed your third year of college and somebody offered you a job managing a hamburger restaurant for $60,000 a year. However you'd be required to leave school. Also suppose you were studying in an area where graduates just out of school had a starting salary of $40,000 a year, but it increased by 20% a year over the next 10 years. Furthermore, it required skills that weren't easy to obtain. What would you do?

In the short-term, the $60,000 a year job looks attractive. After all, you still have to finish another year of college and then wait for over two years before your salary approached $60,000. Over the long-term, however, choosing the hamburger restaurant would be a poor choice. To determine why, let's look at the two options.

First, the restaurant manager's skills are nothing special. There are many qualified people who could do the job. If you were to lose your job for some reason, you'd be competing with too many people for another management job. If you did get one, there is no guarantee you'd be making $60,000 a year. You might have to take a pay cut.

On the other hand, your college degree job doesn't have as many qualified candidates able to do it. Therefore you would be in demand and would most likely be paid an appropriate salary. If you lost that job for some reason, there would be many others from which to choose.

However the biggest advantage is with salaries over 10 years. The restaurant manager would start at $60,000 and because of competition, perhaps receive raises of 2% per year on his already inappropriately high, for the industry, salary. So in the 10th year he would be making a little over $73, 000 a year.

The college graduate would start at $40,000 and end up making over $247,000 a year by the tenth year. In fact by the third year of work, the college grad would be making more than the restaurant manager. And his job would be more secure.

This is an example of the benefits of long-term thinking.

It bears repeating. Building solid wealth is a long-term pursuit. So don't take short-term actions that will hinder your true long-term goals.

By now you should have caught a glimpse of the importance that goals and plans play in your wealth building success. In fact they form the very foundation of your wealth. Choose the wrong goals (or the wrong plans) and even your best efforts can be severely hampered.

If you're to be successful, it's imperative you know the difference between a good goal (and a good plan) and a bad one. Fortunately there's an easy way to ensure you select good goals and implement only good plans.

And that's what we'll discuss in the next chapter.

ACTION PLAN

If you want a dead-simple plan for investing successfully in the stock market and building your wealth with minimum risk, follow these steps.

1) *Find 7 good sector Exchange Traded Funds (ETFs) and 2 or 3 good foreign ETFs or index funds (Chapter Nine describes ETFs).*
2) *Diversify properly using the techniques explained in Chapter Eleven.*
3) *Spend a few hours a month monitoring your investments and rebalancing when necessary.*

That's it! You'll have an investment plan that outperforms the vast majority of actively managed mutual funds, minimizes your risk in the markets and leaves you with plenty of time to pursue activities you enjoy.

Of course you can likely do even better if you spend additional time learning about individual stocks and investing in the exceptional ones (see Chapter Ten). But keep in mind that increased returns don't happen for free. Your risk will probably be greater (although if you follow the guidelines in this book, your risk will still be reasonable) and you'll spend more time managing your investments. However some people gladly accept the tradeoffs .

Chapter Six

Goals and Plans

"If you don't know where you are going, you might wind up someplace else."

Yogi Berra

Emerging from the ancient forest, the barbarian horde swept across the plains, their mighty horses pounding the black sludge beneath their hooves.

Balthazar, the barbarian king, rode at their head, his sword raised and his battle cry echoing off the hills before him. His black steed snorted steam in the chill morning air as thousands of battle hardened warriors thundered after him.

Hate and death shone in each barbarian's eyes as they charged forth in an unthinking frenzy whipped up by the dream of battle and conquest. Hundreds of times, before, had Balthazar led his evil horde into battle and hundreds of times had they completely overwhelmed the opposing forces with their ferocity and savagery.

A thin line of farmers stood on the barren, rocky hills in front of them. Aralon watched as the menacing horde approached. From his vantage point, high above the plains, the barbarians looked like a sea of black death irresistibly creeping towards the hills, devouring everything in its path. Aralon waited.

The line of farmers also waited. Fear welling up in each farmer's heart. Their hands trembled as they clutched their hoes and forks, make-shift weapons they knew were no match for the barbarians' battle-tested steel. Still, they held their line.

Balthazar rode on, his heart pounding in anticipation of the coming victory, the spoils of war, great feasts and tales of glorious battle.

As the last barbarian rider entered the plains, Aralon leapt onto a boulder and waved a red flag with all his might. His signal was repeated by others down the line until many miles away it reached small groups of farmers hiding in the forest behind, and on both sides of, the barbarian horde.

The farmers lit their torches and with a coordinated effort, they thrust them onto the black sludge covering the plains. Flames immediately sprang up and raced quickly across the ground toward the barbarians. The barbarians rode on, unaware of the fiery menace moving up on them.

Aralon waved his flag again. The line of farmers on the hill jumped into action. Using their hoes and forks, they dislodged hundreds of giant boulders, that had been strategically set up beforehand, to form a crushing wall of rolling rock. Balthazar slowed and signaled to his warriors.

With one practiced motion the entire horde turned sharply away from the hills. It was then that Balthazar first noticed something was amiss. Screams of panic could be heard from the rear of his troops.

He swung his horse around and looked back. In the distance he saw a frightening sight. A gigantic wall of flame stood on three sides of the barbarian horde, and it was moving toward them very quickly. "Oil," Balthazar hissed as he looked down at the black sludge covering the plains.

He looked toward the hills. The unyielding wall of stone continued rolling towards him. Balthazar realized, too late, that he was caught between a wall of fire and a wall of stone.

There was nowhere to run. Within seconds the flames spread across the plains. Barbarians screamed as the flames engulfed them. Others panicked and rode away from the fire, only to be crushed beneath the relentless wall of moving stone.

Balthazar and a small contingent managed to evade the stones and head for the hills, barely escaping the flames licking at their flanks. As they started up the hills another onslaught of stone was released. More barbarians fell. Still, Balthazar and most of his elite guard survived.

They continued up the hill only to be set upon by hundreds of farmers wielding hoes and forks. The outnumbered barbarians were no match for the adrenaline-filled farmers. Within moments they were dispatched. As Balthazar lay dying, gasping for breath, he looked back upon his once mighty horde. The plains were engulfed in a raging fiery trap and littered with bodies. Not one barbarian was left standing.

"I love it when a plan comes together," said Aralon.

Had Aralon gone into battle without a well thought out plan, he would have been massacred by the barbarians. Instead he led a group of farmers, inexperienced in battle, to a great victory over a much stronger foe.

And therein lies the benefit of a good plan. A good plan is not an option, it's not a luxury nor is it something to think about if time permits. Rather it is an absolute necessity that must be prepared BEFORE taking action.

Without a plan, all of the best resources and advantages in the world will be for naught. With a plan, even the simplest tools and resources can be combined to produce great benefits.

The Stock Market is somewhat like that barbarian horde. It wields tremendous power and moves forward with a seemingly irresistible force. Too often individuals are caught up in its flow and, unable to escape, quickly overwhelmed.

However it doesn't have to that way. With a good goal, some plans and a few time-tested rules in place, you can escape the clutches of the market monster and thrive in a world littered with the remains of bad investment decisions.

The importance of setting goals and creating plans is so crucial, I'm going to revisit what you need to do.

You already know that if you don't have an investment goal, you won't know where you're going.

To put it into perspective, would you jump into a car, in a strange city, and just follow the road without knowing where it led? If you did that you'd probably find yourself lost and out of fuel. That's why most people have a destination in mind when they start.

Investing is no different. If you don't know what your investment goals are, you're destined to wander aimlessly in the market's wilderness, making one bad decision after another.

By setting your goals, whether it's investing for retirement, your children's college or a three-month family vacation, you can put the appropriate plan into place (such as a long-term, medium-term, or short-term plan).

If you're investing, say, for the long-term, then you can safely ignore short-term market conditions because they won't affect you. However if you don't know your goal, then you won't know whether short-term market fluctuations will affect you or not. That's not a good position to be in.

Once you know your goal you'll need to implement a good plan to get you there.

Many investors lose money because they invest using a hit-and-miss, gut feeling method. They buy and sell when they "feel" it is the right time. Unfortunately "feelings" usually equate to large losses.

Successful investing, like anything else, requires a plan that has been fully researched and historically proven to produce results.

When Toyota builds a car, they use a proven plan that has been refined over the years and has worked for them consistently in the past. They don't build cars based on "feelings." If they did, they'd be out of business very quickly.

ACTION PLAN

Sit down and write out your investment goals. A goal may be something such as, "I want to have $2,000,000 in my retirement account when I retire in 30 years." The more specific your goal, the better. You may have more than one goal, if so write them all down. Remember to be specific.

The next step is to formulate a plan to reach each of your goals - one plan for each goal.

As an example, your plan to reach the goal above might be to start with $10,000 and to realize returns of 20% each year for the next 30 years. That will give you $2,373,762.30.

Once you have the overall plan, break it down into smaller pieces.

So you'll have to determine where to get the initial $10,000. Then you'll have to decide how to make your money grow at a consistent 20% per year. Keep breaking the plan down into smaller and smaller steps until you're able to solve each step.

How important is writing out your goals and developing plans to achieve them? Let's see what super swimmer Michael Phelps had to say after winning his record breaking eighth gold medal at the 2008 Olympics.

"I've dreamt a lot of things, written down a lot of goals and this was the biggest dream I have ever written down... you can imagine anything, to work towards it, through all the ups and downs, to accomplish everything you ever dreamed of, it's fun, it feels pretty good."

It's obvious that Phelps feels he needs to write down his goals in order to transform his dreams into reality. And if you're to do well with your investments, you need to have that same attitude.

Once you've formulated your plans, review them. Ensure they're easy to follow. This is extremely important. Plans that are difficult to follow don't work because people don't follow them.

For example, almost everyone knows how to lose weight (eat sensibly and exercise regularly) but most can't seem to do it.

The reason? Eating right and exercising every day is difficult to do. If people can't do this for their personal health, it's no wonder investment portfolios are in shambles.

If you want to maintain your financial health, ensure your investment plan is easy to follow and not time consuming, or eventually you'll stop using it and go back to your old ways.

You also need to check your plans are reasonable. I've seen some pretty wild investment plans that didn't work – not because they were too difficult to implement, but because they were impossible to implement!

Most of these plans involved making loads of money in the stock market overnight. Stay away from them.

If you had to pick just one reason, trying to get rich quickly would probably be the number one cause of stock market losses. Here's a completely made up example of a get-rich-quick-plan; I call it *Einstein's Sure Fire Way to Millions* because Albert Einstein showed us how to do it.

According to Einstein's theory of Relativity, there is no universal, absolute time. Rather time is a relative thing that is different for people moving uniformly at different speeds. The faster you're moving relative to someone else's frame of reference, the faster your time runs when viewed by that other person.

So, here's what you do.

Go to your broker and deposit $25,000. Put it into an index fund that should return an average of 12% per year.

Then jump into a rocket ship that can fly at 99.5% the speed of light and speed away from earth at full speed. After four years, turn around and come back. When you return, only eight years will have passed for you, however 80 years will have passed on Earth.

Now go back to your broker and cash out. At an average annual rate of 12% you'll have $216,462,077.50. But if we assume inflation will run at 4% a year, then your average annual real rate of return is actually 8%, so you'll have *just* $11,798,870.86 in today's dollars. I haven't taken taxes into consideration, but either way it's still a nice chunk of change that will allow you to retire quite nicely while you're still young.

So what do you think? Do you think it's fanciful? Think it's wishful thinking? Well not according to science. Einstein's theories have been scientifically proven and this plan is theoretically possible, so it's a good plan right?

Well not exactly. The problem, as you've no doubt guessed, is you don't have access to a rocket ship that can fly at 99.5% the speed of light. If you did, you'd have no problem implementing this investment strategy. Unfortunately you don't and the plan depends heavily on the rocket ship. In other words it's a plan that's impossible to achieve.

What I've just described is, on the surface, a plausible strategy (at least if you understand the theory of Relativity it's plausible). It's logical, has scientific backing and is theoretically possible.

However it's not practical because it relies on something that is currently impossible to get – the rocket ship.

That example might seem like nonsense to you, but don't laugh too quickly. A large number of people follow impossible plans, and they pay vast sums of money for the privilege.

There are a multitude of impossible investment strategies out there that sound plausible and may even have scientific backing in some area. But when you dig deeper, when you really look below the surface, you'll find the strategy depends on something that is impossible to do.

It might depend on an indicator that supposedly predicts the market. But that's currently impossible.

Nobody and no indicator can predict the market consistently over the long term. Unfortunately these impossible things aren't usually as blatant and obvious as the missing rocket ship, so they're easy to miss.

Take Technical Analysis and a host of other strategies for instance. They claim to be able to predict the market. But regardless of what they say, they're wrong. They can't consistently predict the market anymore than you or I can by flipping a coin.

Sure it might sound plausible to some, but the reality is it's just another strategy, albeit one that has millions of followers, with a missing rocket ship.

The reason it might sound plausible is that when you think about it, nothing is truly random. Given enough knowledge you can predict anything; from where the ball will drop on the roulette wheel, to a dice roll (given the same starting position with the same angles, energy, external factors and such the dice will turn up the same) to stock price movements.

The problem, however, is, like roulette and rolling dice, we never have enough information to predict stock prices because there are too many unknown variables and/or we can't measure what we need to know accurately enough or within a short enough time period to be useful.

This is what the French mathematician Henri Poincare was getting at when he said, "if we know the causes we can predict the effects. What is chance for the ignorant is not chance for the scientist. Chance is only the measure of our ignorance."

Unfortunately, in the real world we are all ignorant – some are just more ignorant than others.

Current events are always related to past events (cause and effect). Again, the problem is we don't know what the past events are or how they relate to the current event.

This leads to a very profound and useful conclusion when it comes to investing. Peter Bernstein put it best when he wrote, "the essence of risk management lies in maximizing the areas where we have some control over the outcome while minimizing the areas where we have absolutely no control over the outcome and the linkage between effect and cause is hidden from us."

In areas where the linkage is hidden, we have to guess. We can choose to guess in a logical manner, using inductive reasoning or statistics for example, or we can choose to guess illogically by going with our emotions or gut feeling. Buffett, and those like him, choose to guess logically.

They also tend to use abstraction in a way that minimizes needing to know the linkages between effect and cause so that they react in an intelligent manner. The key word here is "react."

Reacting to what the market has done rather than trying to predict the market is the road to riches. To see why, let's look at an example of two equally matched sporting teams.

Would you rather make a bet beforehand and then wait for the outcome, or be able to continually change your bet as the game progresses?

Each time a team scores, you could react by changing your bet. Clearly this reaction strategy would pay off over the long-term much better than the one that requires prediction.

The stock market is similar.

Many investment software packages throw a nice looking GUI on a useless algorithm and suck money from unwitting "investors."

You'd be surprised at how many people design professional looking software with lots of really neat colours, charts and reports, base it on a Moving Average (which does not consistently work for predicting what a stock will do), market it as a way to get rich quickly in the Stock Market and sell it for anywhere from a hundred dollars to thousands of dollars.

And, astonishingly, people buy it.

Before you fall for any of these schemes, always ask yourself, "Where's the rocket ship?"

If someone tries to sell you a system for making hundreds of percent annually or making millions by this time next year, I guarantee you that there is a missing "rocket ship" lurking somewhere in the plan.

But not all impossible plans promise to make you rich quickly. Some might present a realistic goal, such as making a million in 30 years, but nonetheless turn out to be impossible to implement. Therefore you must check and recheck your plans to ensure they will work at a pragmatic level. Don't take any shortcuts here.

Making money is simple, but you must correctly plan for it, ensure all your money is consistently working hard for you and then give it time.

A successful investment portfolio isn't built overnight; it is the result of many years of "doing the right thing" and following a disciplined plan. So remember, if someone tells you they can show you how to make a substantial amount of money in the stock market overnight, run as far away as you possibly can. And be sure to take your chequebook with you.

The get-rich-quick mentality is a popular one because it plays to your emotions (see Chapter Four). But the truth is, there really isn't a way for the average person to make millions overnight.

The risks you must take in order to have a remote chance at making a killing are extremely high. And nobody can do this consistently. In fact, most can't even do it once and very quickly lose their money.

Getting caught up in the hype is only going to delay your true success. Save yourself lots of grief by accepting the fact there is no free lunch.

There are no magical formulas or ancient secrets to profiting quickly in the stock market, but with good goals, solid plans, some time and a little perseverance, almost anyone can do it.

ACTION PLAN

Review your plans and strategies.

Are they achievable? Are they simple enough to follow and do they leave you with plenty of time to do other things? If not, seriously consider changing them. Life is too short to waste your time and effort following plans that are difficult or impossible to implement.

Next, review your current stock holdings. Are they in your portfolio for valid reasons or are they there because you think you'll make a killing any day now?

Consider the risks associated with holding each of your stocks.

Is it probable that the company can go out of business? Can an external force (such as a government agency) ban your company's one product? How will this stock do in a true bear market?

You cannot invest successfully following plans that focus solely on potential returns. You must also carefully consider the risks involved.

Chapter Seven
Time and Compounding

"Compounding is mankind's greatest invention because it allows
for the reliable, systematic accumulation of wealth."

Albert Einstein

C ompounding is the safest and surest way to get rich. And the beauty
of it is that everyone can use it to take care of their financial future.
Another benefit is it's simple. Simple to implement, simple to
understand and simple to explain.

It's a wonder why more people don't use it effectively. I don't think it's
because they don't understand it, rather I think it's because they don't make
the effort to fully see what it can do for them.

After all, you don't need too much intelligence to understand the basic
math involved. And although you do need to stick with your investment plan
day in and day out, if you automate it that's easy enough to do.

No, I think the main reason more people don't use it to their full
advantage is because it starts off slowly and takes time to really get going. But
most people are impatient and want to see immediate results. They don't want
to wait the requisite number of years.

Another reason is it does take some sacrifice – any money you save for
investing can't be spent on consumer goods.

However if you're patient, you'll come to see compounding in a different
light. When you wake up one morning and see how much your investments
have grown (without you having had to work for the profits), compounding
will start to become very interesting. You'll most likely start saving and
investing more too. But it takes time to arrive at that point.

I'll demonstrate the power of compounding with an example.

Let's say we have two young investors, Alice and Bob. Both are 19 years old. Alice opens a tax-deferred plan and immediately begins contributing $2,000 a year for seven years. Alice's returns average 10% annually. After seven years, when Alice is 26, she stops her contributions and never contributes another penny.

Bob, on the other hand, waits until he's 26 years old to start his contributions. He also averages 10% annually in a tax-deferred account, but he contributes $2,000 annually until he's 65.

When both Alice and Bob are 65 years old, who made more money? Your gut will tell you it's Bob, but in fact it is Alice.

Alice would have made $930,641 on her initial investment of $14,000. Bob would have made $893,704 on his initial investment of $80,000.

Table 1 contains the details.

Age	Alice's Contribution	Alice's Portfolio Value	Bob's Contribution	Bob's Portfolio Value
19	$2,000	$2,200	$0	$0
20	$2,000	4,620	$0	$0
21	$2,000	7,282	$0	$0
22	$2,000	10,210	$0	$0
23	$2,000	13,431	$0	$0
24	$2,000	16,947	$0	$0
25	$2,000	20,872	$0	$0
26	$0	22,959	$2,000	$2,200
27	$0	25,255	$2,000	4,620
28	$0	27,780	$2,000	7,282
29	$0	30,558	$2,000	10,210
30	$0	33,614	$2,000	13,431
31	$0	36,976	$2,000	16,947
32	$0	40,673	$2,000	20,872
33	$0	44,741	$2,000	25,159
34	$0	49,215	$2,000	29,875
35	$0	54,136	$2,000	35,062
36	$0	59,550	$2,000	40,762
37	$0	65,505	$2,000	47,045
38	$0	72,055	$2,000	53,950
39	$0	79,261	$2,000	61,545
40	$0	87,187	$2,000	69,899
41	$0	95,905	$2,000	70,089
42	$0	105,496	$2,000	89,198

Age	Alice's Contribution	Alice's Portfolio Value	Bob's Contribution	Bob's Portfolio Value
43	$0	116,045	$2,000	100,318
44	$0	127,650	$2,000	112,550
45	$0	140,415	$2,000	126,005
46	$0	154,456	$2,000	140,805
47	$0	169,902	$2,000	157,086
48	$0	186,892	$2,000	174,995
49	$0	205,581	$2,000	194,694
50	$0	226,140	$2,000	216,364
51	$0	248,754	$2,000	240,200
52	$0	273,629	$2,000	266,420
53	$0	300,992	$2,000	295,262
54	$0	331,091	$2,000	326,988
55	$0	364,200	$2,000	361,887
56	$0	400,620	$2,000	400,276
57	$0	440,682	$2,000	442,503
58	$0	484,750	$2,000	488,953
59	$0	533,225	$2,000	540,049
60	$0	586,548	$2,000	596,254
61	$0	645,203	$2,000	658,079
62	$0	709,723	$2,000	726,087
63	$0	780,695	$2,000	800,896
64	$0	858,765	$2,000	883,185
65	$0	944,641	$2,000	973,704
Total Invested	$14,000	(14,000)	$80,000	(80,000)
Total Profit		$930,641		$893,704

Table 1

That's the power of compounding. But you have to know what to do, take action and then stick to the plan. If you do it the rewards are impressive.

So how can you use the power of compounding to your advantage?

You simply have to learn a few basic rules, implement them and give it time.

So if you're 19 years old and start investing properly right now, you should be able to retire by the time you're in your forties. If you're older, well, people are living much longer nowadays so it's never too late to start.

Here's what you have to do.

1. Convince yourself you can do it. For example if you invest $100 a week at an average annual percentage rate of 12%, after 30 years you'll have $1,540,810.93. Accounting for an average inflation rate of 4% per year, that means you'll have $651,005.43 in today's dollars before taxes. Note that the major indexes have historically returned about 12% a year over a long period of time.

2. Find a comfortable chair and write down your major financial goal. You might write, "I want to retire in 30 years with a million dollars in the bank and no outstanding debts." Be specific. If you have more than one major goal, write them all down.

3. Write a plan, for each goal, that will take you to that specific objective. For example, "I will stop spending wildly, pay off my consumer debt, and then invest 15% of my gross income every month in a vehicle that will achieve an average annual return of 12% over 30 years. Whenever I receive a bonus or unexpected cash windfall, I will invest 50% of it. I will invest only in high-quality companies and I will not, under any circumstances, lose my head chasing the hot stock du jour. I will stick to my plan day in and day out." Again, be very specific.

4. Find the right investment vehicle. This is where you will have to do the lion's share of the work. This is the 20% of the effort that will produce 80% of the results, so ensure you do a good job here. You should only use tested and proven investment methods. The fact you're reading this book means you already have a significant head start.

5. Implement your plan. Once you have your plan, don't wait. Implement it right away. The longer you leave it, the more money you'll lose in lost opportunity.

6. Monitor your plan to ensure it's operating smoothly. You'll most likely have to make minor course corrections along the way, but if you did a good job in step 4, you shouldn't have to spend too much time on monitoring. Using the **Pragmatic Investor** software will help you enormously in this area.

What you have going for you: The best investment resource you have is **Time** and the best investment tool you have is compounding.

Albert Einstein said the magic of compounding was the eighth wonder of the world. But it takes time.

What you have going against you: Thousands of advertisements telling you why you absolutely must spend your hard-earned money on the latest widgets.

What you need: Knowledge (found in this book) and discipline.

Now simply sit back and live your life to the fullest (on 85% of your income and 50% of your bonuses).

In 20 or 30 years, after compounding has done its work, you'll look back and wonder how something so simple managed to escape 95% of the investing public.

Remember, the meaning of true success is the ability to do what you want, **when** you want to do it. And that basically translates into **time**!

Regardless of whether you're broke, building a nest egg, or you're a billionaire named Bill Gates, everyone has the same amount of time each day – 24 hours.

You can't change that and you can't create any more time either. You can, however, spend your time wisely. If you have a plan, there is no reason to worry about what the market will do next.

Whatever it does, your plan should handle it for you.

Investors who spend too much time watching the ticker inevitably let emotions get in the way and end up making costly mistakes.

They waste their precious time and it's usually detrimental, a double whammy. Too many people spend too much time taking too many risks only to end up with below average returns. Don't let that be you. **Don't waste your Time**.

It bears repeating, as an investor your most valuable resource is time – bar none. And yes, time is more valuable than money. And since your time is a limited resource, you will need to learn to use it efficiently. There are certain things that can be automated or safely ignored and others that can't. Spend your time where you have to and automate or ignore everything else. Then let time take over to grow your investments for you automatically.

For example, consider the amount of time you spend watching the ticker, participating in news groups, updating your portfolio, reading market news, following the "experts," and researching the investment environment so you know when to buy and sell.

What are your returns after a year of doing this?

Try keeping a journal for one month and write down exactly how much time you spend on investment related activities. It'll help if you break each activity down into the various tasks.

At the end of the month, add up the totals. It will probably surprise you. You'll see clearly where your time is being spent. Is it being spent on activities that contribute significantly to your returns? If not then you're wasting precious time.

Test all your theories and investment strategies to ensure they are sound. Just because you made a killing on a gut-feeling investment, doesn't mean it's a good strategy.

Your strategy will have to consistently give you above average returns over the long-term. If it doesn't then you're better off investing in an index fund.

One of the biggest myths circulating today is you can make all your investment decisions using information available on the Web and clean up in the stock market. Don't believe the hype, and don't waste your time trying to do it.

It doesn't work because millions of other people have access to that very same information. Not only that, but you're competing against professionals with large research departments and even larger budgets.

One of the most important things you can ever do is to implement a disciplined, proven strategy and stick with it. But ensure it doesn't take too much of your valuable time or you'll either stop using it or you won't have time for the more important things in life.

ACTION PLAN

Keep a journal for one or two months and then analyze how much of your time is spent doing necessary tasks and how much is wasted.

The rule of thumb is that 20% of the work provides 80% of the results.

Ensure you're focusing on the 20% of the work that really counts.

Chapter Eight
The Best Ideas

"A man should look for what is, and not for what he thinks should be."

Albert Einstein

O lder ideas that have been around and withstood the test of time as well as peer reviews, and challenges from others, should be given more credibility than new ideas that sound good but have not withstood the test of time.

Sometimes new ideas have such merit they literally change an entire field overnight. Einstein's ideas on Relativity did just that in theoretical physics and the Internet did it to pretty much everything else. But like Muhammad Ali and Michael Jordan, these are exceptionally rare occurrences.

Most of the time new ideas don't bring anything revolutionary, in and of themselves, to the table. The power of new ideas is they gradually build upon one another over time and eventually transform their fields without anyone ever really noticing.

It's much like cooking a frog by turning up the heat ever so slowly so he doesn't realize he's being cooked.

Unfortunately the terms "old" and "old-fashioned," have taken on an almost derogatory meaning. That's too bad, because when it comes to investing, "old-fashioned" is still the way to go.

Old-fashioned concepts, that have been around for thousands of years (such as buying low and selling high), still make you money.

The methods we now have at our disposal to implement these concepts have changed dramatically, but the concepts themselves haven't.

Yet people ignore sound concepts and focus on the methods as if the methods were the goal rather than just a means to the goal. For example, how many investors read daily investment Newspapers or look at stock market shows on television? Millions and Millions is my guess.

But most of that time is wasted. Most of that News is simply noise that cause stock prices to overreact (either by falling too low or rising too high) for no good reason.

Over the long-term, this noise is reduced by such a degree that it is overtaken by the true value of the stock.

As time goes by, the new noise has less and less of an effect on a particular investment because it causes the stock price to move less and less relative to when it was originally purchased.

For example, if you bought a stock at $5 twenty years ago and it is now trading at $300, then the fact that noise, today, causes that stock to lose 10% of its value is less of a worry to you than it is to someone who purchased it today at $300.

You're more likely to take a long-term outlook, and ignore the noise, because you haven't just lost 10% of your initial investment.

So if reading or listening to financial News doesn't help you with your investments or help you in some other area of your life, then it is simply wasted time (unless you read it solely for its entertainment value).

And since everyone, even Warren Buffett, has only 24 hours in a day, it's probably a good idea to stop wasting your time and instead use it constructively.

And that usually means following a plan that has been tested properly over time.

Following newly created plans is akin to being on the leading edge (and in some cases, the bleeding edge).

The problem with this strategy is you really don't know if the new plan will work. History suggests the majority of new plans fail.

So the probability is you will fail.

And the downside is not merely the failure, but the fact you may not know you've failed until it is far too late to implement the correct plan – which could lead to unrecoverable financial loss.

Many times a new theory might sound good, but until you actually use it, until you try to apply it in a real-world situation, you won't know if it will truly work.

That's why I continue to recommend going with tested and proven plans that have been around long enough to work out the inevitable bugs, and why I suggest leaving the new plans alone.

If, in 20 years, one of the new plans of today proves itself, then perhaps you could use it. Until then, the best strategy is to stick with the tried and true.

But why do the majority of new plans fail? It's simple really: there are too many variables to take into account, and new plans tend to ignore or inaccurately incorporate some important ones. But it's not just the standard variables, it's also the unknowns introduced by other people.

When investing, you can't apply knowledge in isolation, unaware of what others are doing. Rather you need to make choices based on how others are currently acting. An entire field, called game theory, has evolved to study this and it is very complicated. Some of the brightest mathematical minds devote their entire careers to it and it's changed the way we view uncertainty. The major insight brought to us by game theory is that a major source of uncertainty lies with what others plan to do.

So even if, overcoming all probability, a new plan is actually a good one in and of itself, there's a good chance it might fail when forced to interact with what people are currently doing in the real world.

The fact remains, even with the quantity and quality of research available today, when it comes to the market, you still don't have enough information to know exactly what everyone else is thinking or doing.

You can't even abstract it in order to have a slight chance of wrapping your mind around it.

It's just too complex a problem.

So not only can't you predict where the market will go, but you can't predict how new strategies will perform in the future and thus your choices will most likely be sub-optimal.

Before we move on, let's talk a bit about abstraction. Abstraction can be good. But it can also be a trap.

Think of our human senses. They are limited in what they can perceive and for the most part that's a good thing.

Imagine if your eyes had quantum resolution and could see things at the quantum level. You'd see every sub-atomic, atomic and molecular movement.

But unless your brain increased proportionally to handle this extra information, you'd be overwhelmed.

However most of the quantum-level behaviour is cancelled out at the macro level (so for our part, much of it can be construed as just noise in that it doesn't impart useful information to us).

Therefore you can see, in this case, the fact your senses have a relatively low resolution is good. The smaller details are hidden from you and abstracted into simpler macro forms (such as trees, houses, grains of sand and such).

Unfortunately when we make the jump to investing there is a drawback. Sometimes we take abstraction too far and lose important information that hampers our decision-making and causes us to make bad choices.

At the other extreme, if we increase the resolution too much when we look at the market (for example, looking at a stock price every second rather than every month), we increase the probability that what we're seeing is just noise and therefore we're apt to make faulty decisions based on the noise rather than the true information.

Over time, market noise tends to cancel out (much like quantum behaviour cancels out at the macro level) and the true value generally dominates – but it takes time for this to occur.

Add to this the tendency of a loss causing more psychological pain than a win, and you can see the rationality for not micromanaging your portfolio by looking at too high a resolution.

Ideally you want to view the market at as low a resolution (that is, as high an abstraction) as you can without losing any pertinent information. But that's more difficult than it sounds.

Back in the prehistoric days, things were much simpler. Not better mind you, but simpler. Back then it was possible for a smart caveman to know pretty much everything that affected him. He was more insulated from external forces.

Sure there was the occasional ice age or dearth of game, but all in all our caveman friends were in control of their own destinies. Nobody halfway around the world could influence them. They hunted, they ate, and they slept. They also died at a very early age.

Conversely, modern developed economies have allowed people to live long and live well. Never, in the history of mankind, have people had such a high standard of living or life expectancy as those in today's first world nations. But these benefits do not come without a price, and that price is complexity.

Today there is nobody who can understand everything that affects him in our developed economies. However the benefits far outweigh the costs, so most people are generally happy with our progress – which is evidenced by the fact I don't know of anyone who would rather live in the prehistoric era, even if life was simpler back then.

According to William Bernstein, in his book, "The Birth of Plenty," human progress depends on four things: property rights, scientific rationalism, capital markets and transportation/communication.

Speaking about capital markets, he states, "Entrepreneurs must have access to sufficient capital to pursue their visions."

It goes without saying that capital is provided to those that use it efficiently at better terms than to those who don't. Inefficient capital users must pay more for capital, if they can get it at all.

But how do investors know who is using capital efficiently? Many years ago, before laws and agencies were created to enforce accurate and timely reporting of a company's financial condition, it was difficult to assess how effectively a company used its capital.

Was its capital building a sound business? Or was it going to line the head honcho's pockets? Even today, there's no doubt some high-level executives find ways to skirt the laws and line their pockets with investors' money; however it is far more difficult to do so now than at any point in the past.

So concentrating on the normal case, that being timely and accurate reporting of a company's financial health, it is clear investors have access to the data they need to determine who is using capital effectively and who is not. But a problem still remains.

Having access to data is not the same thing as being able to parse the data and understand it. Data in corporate reports must be laboriously extracted and interpreted and then compared to other data, such as those from previous years and/or different companies.

If you think about it, good investors make their money by comparing companies and selecting the best ones based on financial data and capital usage. But the effort required to sift through the jumble of corporate results and come to accurate conclusions is staggering. What should be completely automated is currently done manually, or at most, only slightly automated.

And while professional investors have large staffs that do the grunt work for them, small investors must either do this themselves (a practically insurmountable task) or settle for selecting from a small subset of stocks (those they have the time to analyze).

It's no wonder many small investors don't bother analyzing company fundamentals – it's just too tedious and time consuming, but it's also very risky.

Now it is not generally possible to evaluate every single piece of corporate data in order to draw conclusions on whether to invest or not.

However it is entirely possible for investors to abstract these data and draw conclusions from the abstracted results. That's the reason common ratios, such as P/E and the Current Ratio, were invented.

When used correctly they help investors interpret the data and make sound investment decisions.

But with what should these ratios be compared? What's a "good" P/E? What's a "bad" Current Ratio?

Thankfully a number of people have developed heuristics (or rules of thumb), based on their experiences over the years, that can be used to define what's "good" and "bad." Benjamin Graham was one such person.

Graham arrived at a set of heuristics he published in his book, "The Intelligent Investor." In it he laid out what he thought certain key financial ratios and information should be.

Others have also contributed in this area. This, combined with the ubiquitous availability of corporate data – thanks to the Internet, now allowed investors the unprecedented ability to perform their own analysis on most companies. But there was STILL something missing.

Although abstraction eased some of the tedious calculations and analysis, it didn't eliminate them completely. Investors now had to analyze these abstracted data and apply the correct heuristics to them (quite an improvement over having to analyze the underlying data, but still terribly boring and time consuming).

What was needed was a way to automatically evaluate the relevant abstracted data and report whether the company was worth considering or not.

All of the pieces were there. The Internet, online financial reports and the proven and time-tested research and heuristics thanks to people such as Ben Graham, Warren Buffett, Bill Sharpe and Harry Markowitz – among others.

The missing ingredient was the thread that would stitch all of these individual pieces together, and this thread was software.

Professionals were already using software to help them make better investment decisions. However individual investors were not – or if they were, the majority were using programs based on strategies that weren't proven and didn't work.

Software that was powerful enough to let investors take advantage of fundamental analysis, diversification, asset allocation, portfolio optimization and rebalancing, yet was easy to use and relatively inexpensive was just not available.

And that's why the Pragmatic Investor software was created. It was created to fill this exact need.

It takes the tedium out of the investment process and reduces the inevitable errors associated with manually performing the required calculations.

And since it was built on strategies that were already tested and proven, it just worked.

And that's really how the best ideas evolve. They build on the solid foundation of previously proven systems but add their own advantages to the mix without negating any of the previous advantages.

ACTION PLAN

Visit PragmaticInvestor.com and take the guided video tour of the software.

You'll find it helps you easily implement the ideas and strategies you're learning about in this book

---

Chapter Nine

The Stock Market

"I never blame myself when I'm not hitting. I just blame the bat and if it keeps up, I change bats. After all, if I know it isn't my fault that I'm not hitting, how can I get mad at myself?"

Yogi Berra

Harrison Ford once said, "One day I called George Lucas up at three o'clock in the morning and I pretended to be Mark Hamill. He said, 'Harrison?'
I said 'No, it's me Mark Hamill.'
He said, 'Harrison, I know it's you.'
I said, 'Well then you know wrong because it's Mark Hamill.'
He sighed and said, 'okay Mark what do you want?' I really got him."

What's interesting about this is that some people play this game with the stock market.

They'll suspect what they're doing is completely wrong, because they're continually losing money in (or under-performing) the market, but they'll keep telling the market, and anyone who will listen, that what they're doing is right.

When others point out the facts, they'll insist the others are mistaken. Finally everyone will stop listening and simply, sigh, nod in agreement and say, "okay." The "investor" will then take that as a sign that he's right and continue down his chosen path to his detriment. The market, on the other hand, will carry on its merry way, uninterested in any single investor's delusional view.

So why would ordinarily intelligent people behave this way? Could it be human nature gumming up the works again? Absolutely!

While most people wouldn't try to build their own house, without first going to school and then apprenticing for a few years, these same people think it's fine to build their own wealth in an ad-hoc manner. Why? Because building a house gives instant feedback. If you don't lay the foundation correctly, you'll know when the frame comes tumbling down. There's no rationalizing your way out of that situation.

On the other hand, building wealth doesn't give the same kind of feedback. If you lose money, it's easy to rationalize that it wasn't your fault, it was the market's. Further, the completed product is so far into the future, the feedback is not as immediate as with building a house.

So you can go about your wealth-building endeavors under the illusion you're doing it correctly because you won't find out you're wrong for many long years. The fact there's also numerous investment tools available help to support this misconception.

Just because you can use a tool doesn't mean you're using it correctly. Not to mention some tools are just plain useless. However because you have access to these tools, it can make you feel as if you know what you're doing. This can be disastrous.

Tools don't absolve you from controlling your life.

Tools should make it easier to accomplish your goals, but they don't accomplish them for you. You still have to take control and know what you're doing.

Yet the illusion persists that if you're using a tool, everything will be all right. It can be, but it's by no means guaranteed. And where do you think the greatest number of new investment tools are located?

If you guessed the Internet, you're right. And because the vast majority of investors are new to the game, they have very little long-term experience in the stock market.

During the Internet boom it was easy. Pick a stock (the exact one really didn't matter, just as long as it had "high-tech" attached to it – or better yet, "Internet"), invest everything you could come up with and wait a few weeks – a month at most. Then sell and pocket a tidy profit. It didn't matter which tool you were using, in fact it didn't matter whether you used a tool at all, everything came out smelling like roses.

However after the boom ended, we saw these same can't-miss stocks plummet to 52-week lows and beyond. Margin calls increased dramatically and many investors lost 50% or more of their capital.

It's no secret that in a rapidly rising market everyone looks like a genius. The trick is how you do over the long term. Investing by the seat of your pants, relying on emotions, and planning for a short-term killing is akin to playing the lottery, and equally as futile.

Study after study has shown that in the long run, emotional investing, which leads to thoughts of "getting rich quick," rarely works. In fact those same studies have shown this kind of investing technique is an almost sure way to lose money. Add to that the usual response of selling when the market dives and most people would be better off putting their money in guaranteed certificates.

The sad part is people don't like guaranteed instruments because they aren't exciting. There's no thrill. Personally, I think if you want thrills, go skydiving or bungee jumping. If you want to invest, then do it properly – and that means the less thrills the better.

This of course begs the question of how to go about it properly. The Internet is a great starting point and has opened the door to the investment realm for millions of people. But in doing so it has created a new set of problems. With so much information available, it becomes increasingly difficult to filter the good from the bad.

But there's a more subtle trap.

The Internet has given the average person the tools to invest, but not necessarily the knowledge or the discipline to do it wisely. So even if the tool is good, it might be used incorrectly – perhaps with devastating results.

I've seen so many people get their hands on investment tools and then proceed to misuse them. And the sad part is that they don't realize how it will affect their portfolios in the future. They seem to feel that just because they have the tool, they're qualified to use it.

To truly grasp the absurdity of this, let's look at an example. I have a friend who's a pilot for a major U.S. Airline. He has flown thousands upon thousands of hours and constantly attends training to keep his skills up to date. Even so he's limited to flying one type of aircraft at a time.

Now let's suppose the government suddenly decided to open the friendly skies and let everyone who was interested take an airplane out for a spin. No training, no minimum level of competence, and no pilot's license required. If you think you can fly, take a plane up. My feeling is that most people would think this was insane – especially those who lived near airports. There would also be a marked increase in plane crashes. Nobody in his or her right mind would support this.

But that's exactly what the investment industry has done with the Internet. Anyone can open a brokerage account and start trading. No training, no minimum level of competence, and no license required. Yet most people think this is a good idea. Nobody calls it absurd.

And best of all, you don't hear about the crashes. Rest assured, however, they're out there.

Investment principles haven't changed in the past 100 years. Investment methods have changed, but the underlying, fundamental principles remain the same.

Principles such as performing your own fundamental analysis, investing in high-quality companies, diversifying over different asset classes, doing your due diligence, buying low and selling high, ignoring your emotions and the list goes on and on.

The methods we now have available to implement these principles are vastly different than what we had even 10 years ago. But some people believe because the methods have changed, the basic principles have too.

The bad news is the market will punish anyone who chooses to believe this fairy tale. Contrary to popular belief, a company has to have good earnings potential and make a profit – whether they're an Internet company or not and whether they were founded 100 years ago or two months ago.

The number one problem with investors today is their lack of knowledge. Right there in second place, however, is their lack of discipline.

Even investors who have the knowledge constantly succumb to the temptation of their emotions. When markets are rapidly rising, greed fuels the belief that the trend will go on forever. People who make 40% in one week tend to extrapolate this over many years – basking in the glory of how much their portfolio will be worth five or ten years hence.

In fact they borrow money, usually by way of margin, to increase their potential returns. Consequently when the markets turn, they're the first to sell. Either because of margin calls or, more commonly, fear. So they buy high and sell low. Common sense will tell you that's not the way to make money.

Unfortunately this phenomenon isn't new. It's always been possible to lose vast sums of money in the stock market, but the Internet now allows you to lose your money faster than ever before.

Many baby boomers are thinking of retirement for the first time in their lives and can't see how their current savings will meet their retirement needs. They know they need to be in the stock market, but they don't know how to go about it. So they jump into the market and make mistake after mistake. Sadly, most don't have the time to recover from even one major error.

Deciding what to do can be a time consuming task. However it's time well spent. Some people will put more effort into choosing a moderately priced car than in thinking about their investments – investments that are supposed to take them comfortably through the rest of their lives. That's not much different than taking off in a 747 when you don't know what you're doing.

"But wait," you might be thinking, "I'm okay! I wouldn't jump on something as crazy as the Internet bandwagon or use an investment tool incorrectly.

That's why I invested in mutual funds with some of the largest fund companies. I've got professionals managing my money, that's pretty smart, right?"

Wrong.

Certain types of mutual funds are terrific, others, especially the actively managed ones, are atrocious.

The reason is that actively managed mutual funds are the equivalent of investing for the uninformed.

It's startling to see that the measure of investment success in almost all of these funds is based on how many times a manager can beat the indexes.

It should be obvious that the goal of investing is to make money, not beat indexes. A manager should be measured by his success in what he's trying to accomplish – and that is to make money.

A hypothetical manager who beats the indexes 14 years in succession, but makes significantly less money than one who beats the indexes only 5 of the 14 years should not be viewed as superior.

At the end of the day, it's the amount of profit made that counts. The problem is how investment firms market success and how easily investors buy into these marketing schemes.

Trying to consistently beat the market by focusing on short-term profits, at the expense of doing the right thing long-term, is counterproductive; however since most managers count on their year-end bonuses (which is obviously a short-term measure) to fund the lifestyle to which they've become accustomed, they have no incentive to choose the most efficient long-term strategy.

Rather they tend to pick strategies that are least likely to fail in the short-term. Essentially, the penalty for looking bad in the short-term is far, far worse (from their perspective) than the penalty for severely underperforming the markets long-term.

So they sacrifice substantial long-term performance in order to meet short-term objectives.

You cannot invest for the long-term using short-term strategies in much the same way you can't win a marathon by implementing 100-meter sprinting techniques.

As an example, consider a fund manager who finds a good undervalued stock and buys it. It then takes 5 years before the rest of the market discovers this stock is a good buy.

When the market catches on, however, the stock explodes in price realizing staggering returns – but during the 5-year period, it under-performs its market index.

Another manager chases the latest hot stocks and buys and sells them over the same 5 years. Each year (against the odds as we'll see later) he manages to beat the index, just barely, and is thus touted as an investment genius.

However at the end of 5 years, the first manager's sound fundamental strategy makes substantially more money than the second's short-term strategy. Which Manager would you rather have managing your retirement funds?

What's worse is that over 80% of actively managed mutual funds don't beat the market. Their managers sacrifice long-term performance trying to beat the market using short-term strategies and 80% of them can't even do that.

If you're going to spend 40 years working hard at a job you don't really like, you might as well spend a few hours each month following some good plans in order to grow your wealth and generate passive income rather than entrusting your money to people who have a documented and proven track record of **underperforming the market**, on average, and charging you exorbitant fees for doing so.

You don't even have to go back very far to witness just how blatant the fund companies' marketing has become.

Back in the heady days of the Internet boom, it wasn't uncommon to see full-page advertisements, in the financial sections of major newspapers, touting the monstrous gains made by a company's mutual funds in the past year.

I can remember seeing just such an ad proclaiming an 85% increase in value. Of course there was nothing in the ad, I even checked the fine print, showing the fund's long-term performance, and there was a disclaimer, conveniently hidden in the small print, that stated past returns were no guarantee of future returns. However the implication was clear, invest in this fund and you'll enjoy 85% returns this year, next year and well into the future.

I can just imagine all of the people that took out their calculators trying to determine how much their nest egg would be worth ten years hence… "let's see, $25,000 times 1.85 times 1.85 times 1.85… and that comes to $11,739,706." As we now know, things didn't exactly turn out that way, but that same fund company is still giving advice, selling funds and making money.

That's the beauty of being a fund company; it makes money whether markets go up or down. Individual investors bear all the risk and fund companies make all the profits. If investors lose money, fund companies still make a profit. If investors are lucky enough to make a profit, fund companies make a bigger profit.

Because of this, mutual fund companies don't like you to know how much you're paying them. After all, if you don't know, it's infinitely less likely you'll go off and start comparing things, things that can only lead to embarrassing questions like, "why am I paying you so much to under-perform the market?" So fund companies silently take out fees and expenses during the year.

You'll never receive a bill asking you to pay for last year's fees. That would be too inconvenient – not to mention eye opening for the fund investor. Instead you'll receive information that hides fees and expenses behind very small numbers as if to imply you're not really paying that much. "Our fund's Management Expense Ratio (MER) is a measly 2% of assets, 2% is not a very big number after all."

Unfortunately the size of a number is a relative thing. Take the numbers 1 and 1,000,000 for example. Most people would think 1 is small and 1,000,000 is large.

However it really depends on what the numbers represent. For instance, a million miles is extremely small when measuring the universe, but one mile is rather large if you have to run that distance over hot coals in your bare feet.

Similarly 2% might be considered small when talking about election results but it's not so small when you consider you're losing 2% of your assets each year. And if you reframe it in light of your potential gains it looks uglier – much uglier.

The S&P 500 has historically returned an average of about 11% per year. If your fund company is taking 2% of your total assets, that means it's taking about 20% of your expected average gain. Worse still, if your fund loses money in a particular year, the fund company still gets paid. So you lose money on your capital and you lose an extra bit of money to the fund company.

But it doesn't even stop there. When you add trading expenses, audit fees and redemption fees, the picture gets much worse – for you, not the fund company.

But don't think that's all. They're not finished with you yet. Many funds pass additional expenses on to you using what is known as, "soft dollars." This is where they pay inflated commissions on their trades to the brokerage firms and receive rebates in the form of free research, hardware and software tools, office space subsidies, magazine subscriptions and other goodies that should be coming out of the MER they charge. Since you pay for trading fees separate from and in addition to the MER, this is a sneaky (but perfectly legal) way to get you to pay for expenses you most likely think are covered by the, already high, MER.

Of course the standard mutual fund wisdom is that costs aren't so important as long as your overall performance is good. And with professional money managers working night and day on your behalf, you're much more likely to outperform the market.

But is this really true? As it turns out, the answer is a resounding "No!"

According to a study by John Bogle, the legendary founder of Vanguard, over the past 15 years, "the average actively managed stock mutual fund returned approximately 3.2% less per year to its shareholders than the stock market returns in general."

To put it into perspective, if you had invested $100 a week for 30 years and received an average annual return of 10% rather than 13.2% (after subtracting the 3.2% by which the average fund under-performs the market), your portfolio would be worth **$1,030,537.20 less**.

That's a very significant difference. It's more than **one million dollars** coming directly out of your pocket.

During that same period, Bogle found that large-cap funds under-performed their benchmark by 2.9% annually, small-cap funds under-performed by 2% and mid-caps under-performed by a whopping 4.7%.

Moreover Bogle found only 9 of 355 actively managed equity funds beat their benchmarks over a period of 30 years. That's a paltry 2.5%. And there was no way of knowing which nine would outperform until after the fact.

In another study covering 1984 to 2002, he found that actively managed mutual funds, taken as a group, on average returned just 9.3% compared to the S&P 500's 12.2%. However individuals who invested in these mutual funds averaged, wait for it, a trifling 2.6%. So not only did the mutual funds underperform the market, but individual mutual fund investors **significantly** underperformed the underperforming mutual funds!

How can this be?

The answer goes back to our discussion on emotions. These investors were impulsive, chasing the latest "hot" fund and jumping into funds that had recently done well. When these funds declined (after all, a fund cannot indefinitely stay hot), they sold and purchased the new "hot" fund. In short, they consistently bought high and sold low.

They also tried to time the market and succumbed to many of the other psychological biases we discussed earlier. And the result? An average 2.6% annual return from 1984 to 2002.

But Bogle wasn't alone in his findings. A study by Robert Jeffrey and Robert Arnott looked at 71 large-cap actively managed funds from 1982 to 1991 and found that only 2 managed to beat the S&P 500 index. And again, it wasn't possible to pick those 2 in advance.

So how do fund companies get otherwise intelligent people to pay so much for so little? In addition to ignorance, the secret is greed and fear.

By cherry picking after the fact, fund companies can continually advertise funds that significantly outperform the market. But if you pay attention you'll notice these funds magically change with each new advertisement. One month it might be the technology fund, the next it might be the precious metals fund and the month after that it might be the bond fund.

Of course the one constant will always be the fund company's logo. The casual observer will only remember that fund company ABC had advertisements expounding the fact their funds had significantly outperformed the markets 12 months running. The actual individual fund's long-term performance numbers will be absent. That's the greed part of it. Promise market beating returns day in and day out but obscure the actual details.

The fear part is to create the illusion that investing is time-consuming, difficult, requires lots of knowledge and is inherently risky if you don't know what you're doing – "and by the way Mr. Investor," they'll imply, "you most certainly do not know what you're doing."

Now while all of these things can be true, they don't have to be.

The fund companies' point is that investing on your own is not a good idea because investing is complicated, time-consuming and risky.

Why? Because *they say so.*

But paying 20% of your average gains, and paying even when you have a losing year, in order to under-perform the market, on average, is (and this is the tricky bit to follow) a great idea.

And as we've seen, fund managers are rated, and receive their bonuses, based on their short-term performance. So a fund manager has a powerful incentive to enhance his short-term performance and make it look like he'd long ago picked the best performing stocks – hence the term "window dressing." Unfortunately, what's usually good in the short-term is bad in the long-term. And most investors are in for the long term.

But long-term, the fund manager will probably be gone, and if he's still around, who'll remember what he did 15 years ago? Short-term, he needs to keep his job and get that big bonus. So if you were in his shoes, what would you do?

Think about this. The average investor can invest successfully, and spend less than one hour a month on his investments, by buying the right kinds of Exchange Traded Funds (ETFs).

Like traditional mutual funds, ETFs aggregate a variety of stocks into one basket. So instead of purchasing all of the individual securities that make up the basket separately, you can purchase a single security. Unlike traditional funds, however, ETF shares can be purchased and sold like regular stocks throughout the trading day. There are no redemption restrictions whatsoever. In some cases you can also use margin and sell short – if desired.

ETFs also come in a variety of flavors. You'll find ETFs that track broad indexes such as the S&P 500, the Nasdaq 100 and the Dow, but you'll also find ETFs that track specific sectors. Sector ETFs have the greatest advantage, as you'll see, because they allow you to diversify by sector and take advantage of the lower correlations that exist between specific sectors.

In addition, ETFs allow you to diversify into foreign markets without having to learn about specific foreign companies because there are ETFs available that track major foreign indexes. Since foreign markets usually have relatively low correlation with the North American markets, it makes sense to invest some of your funds in those markets. Other advantages?

ETFs provide instant diversification, low Management Expense Ratios (MERs average about 0.2%), can be more tax efficient than actively managed funds and they eliminate the difficulty of picking individual securities.

Investors can learn everything they need to know about ETFs in a few hours – and once they have that knowledge, it's with them forever. Finally, diversifying over a few different types of ETFs can further minimize risk.

So spending a few hours researching ETFs and then investing in a few good ones that properly diversify your assets over different sectors will reap significant benefits in the future. You'll pay far less in fees and expenses and you'll most likely outperform your current actively managed funds in the long run.

Remember, buying a mutual fund is a good thing as long as its total expenses (not just the MER) are low and you're sufficiently, but not overly, diversified.

That means you should limit your selections to index funds and sector ETFs – regardless of how much those heavily advertised, actively managed funds are hyped.

"But what about Warren Buffett? He ran an actively managed fund and made his investors rich?"

That's true. But Buffett didn't run one as large as today's average fund. However that's not even the point. The point is that he's Warren Buffett and the fund managers working for the big fund companies aren't.

If you follow hockey, you'll know that Bobby Orr was the greatest defenceman to ever play the game. Before Orr, defencemen never made forays into the offensive zone. Rather they stayed back on defence.

However Orr changed all that by making end-to-end rushes and scoring more goals than many of the forwards in his era. He was able to do this because he was an exceptional skater and could anticipate when he could go and when he should stay back.

His skating ability and speed allowed him to get back to his defensive position even when he lost the puck in the offensive zone.

At the other end of the spectrum was a defenceman named Dave Babych. Even if you're a hockey fan you might not have heard of Dave Babych (he played for the Vancouver Canucks).

The reason is he was as slow as molasses and watching him was anything but exciting. If he decided to make a rush into the other zone (which he never did), I'm sure he'd lose the puck, but if by some miracle he didn't lose it and garnered a shot on net, he wouldn't be able to get back into position quickly enough to do his job. That's the difference between Orr and Babych.

And while most fund managers would like to believe they're the investment equivalents of Bobby Orr, they're usually a bunch of Dave Babychs. Whereas a guy like Buffett *is* a Bobby Orr. So just because he made his investors rich doesn't mean it'll happen to you in a fund run by a mere Dave Babych.

"Okay, actively managed mutual funds are out. But what about options? I heard you can make a killing."

Indeed you can. You can also lose lots of money. Your money.

Here's what James Cramer has to say about options, "The first thing you've got to know about buying options is that you are expected to lose money. It's like the slot machines at the casino. Some people hit; most people lose. Just like in slots, you don't think you should be a loser."

I agree. If you want to trade options, it's your money and thus your call. However I'd strongly recommend that you don't, especially if you're just starting out. You can do very well without them and your risk will be significantly less.

Options require you to be right about the market's direction as well as the time frame. You also need to be right about interest rates and volatility. That's quite a few things you need to be right about. If you're wrong on any of these things, you can lose your money.

"Okay, no options. What about shorting a stock?"

The same thinking applies. Let's take your car for example.

There is absolutely nothing you can do to ensure someone doesn't break into your car. The best alarms, locks and other security devices don't guarantee that your car is 100% impenetrable.

However if you know there will be other cars parked near yours, you can certainly make your car much less attractive to thieves by making it more difficult to break into. Usually a thief will then bypass your car and move to one that's easier.

Similarly it's not impossible to make money shorting a stock, it's just more difficult and the risks are greater. And while I don't mean to equate an investor with a thief, investors can certainly learn something from thieves.

If there are two alternatives that will allow you to reach your goal, go with the easier one. And that means most investors should avoid shorting stocks.

"So no options, no shorting, what about Margin? Can I use Margin?"

Of course you can. But again, there are risks of which you need to be aware. Margin is a double-edged sword. If things go right, you can magnify your returns because you've effectively used leverage to your advantage.

The downside is that you can also magnify your losses if the market moves against you. So unless you fully understand the risks involved, unless you have enough cash in reserve to cover any margin calls, you should stay away from margin.

But there is one strategy that can be employed with relatively little risk (but it is still riskier than not using margin). If you use margin to move money between stocks when your preferred entry and exit prices don't exactly correspond, it can be beneficial.

For example, say you're fully invested in stock A and you've decided to sell your position in A when the share price reaches $10 in order to purchase a position in stock B. But you want B's share price to fall to $20 before you buy.

Let's say stock B does indeed hit your $20 target price but stock A languishes at $9. In that case, you could use margin to purchase shares of stock B at $20 without having to sell stock A at $9. Then when stock A eventually hits your target price of $10, sell it and pay off the margin balance.

That's one example of the judicious use of margin. Using margin to load up on a speculative issue because your boss's, friend's cousin heard it'll go through the roof next week is not a good way to use margin. Use your common sense.

"But my broker says…" hold it right there! The first thing you need to realize is your broker is not on your side. It's true. Brokers are really salesmen and many don't know much about prudent investing or how to properly analyze company fundamentals.

You'd do well to always remember that brokers are trying to sell you something and filter their advice accordingly.

But there's another reason to be wary of brokers bearing good news about stocks.

Most brokerages have an investment banking arm and a retail arm (where your broker works). The investment banking arm is responsible for getting companies to fork over truckloads of cash (through fees on IPOs, debt offerings and other means). In exchange they raise cash for the company by selling its securities to public investors.

The investment bank doesn't necessarily care about the quality of the company, just that the company can pay its fees.

In fact, the companies most likely to need the services of an investment bank are those that are short on cash. So it's not too difficult to picture a situation where an investment bank is hired to raise funds for a company with less-than-average prospects.

Now do you think it would be easier to raise capital, in other words sell new shares, for a company that has a strong buy rating on its stock or a sell rating? Keep that answer in mind for a moment.

Let's say there's a company that's very short on cash. We'll call it "Too Much Debt Inc." (ticker 2MD). If the investment bank is trying to woo 2MD and one of the bank's analysts happened to rate 2MD's stock as a strong buy, how do you think 2MD's executives will feel about that investment bank? Would they be more inclined to throw them some business? You bet they would. And they do! And what happens after the investment bank has the business and is trying to sell 2MD's stock? Would that strong buy rating help? You answered that one in the last paragraph.

Okay, the investment bank now has a large quantity of less than stellar shares to unload, what can it do? One option is to have a research analyst, who incidentally works for the SAME brokerage company, write something nice about the stock and give it a great recommendation.

But wait! What about the low quality stock offering? How in the world does the investment bank get an analyst, who's livelihood just happens to depend on keeping his job at the brokerage, to say a stock that is a terrible investment is actually a good buy?

I'll leave that one up to you.

So what ends up happening is the analyst writes a great recommendation and it lands on, you guessed it, your broker's desk – who incidentally works for the SAME brokerage company as the analyst, which is in fact the SAME company that owns the investment bank.

Now your broker usually receives commissions on each trade, so his compensation increases as the number, and size, of trades in your account increase.

If he can get you to purchase shares of 2MD, he makes money. And his job is made easier with that glowing analyst's report he can wave under your nose.

So he makes money, the investment bank makes money by taking a percentage of the proceeds and the analyst takes home a large bonus at the end of the year. Everyone is happy... even you, at least for the moment, who's stuck with a bad stock and don't even know it.

Bottom line? Don't take advice from a broker! Period. It doesn't hurt to listen, sometimes, but do your own thinking.

Until brokers are compensated based on the long-term performance of their clients' portfolios, rather than on trading frequency, they will have no incentive to recommend trades that are profitable for you.

Rather they will attempt to maximize their income by having you trade more frequently. And it won't matter to them what you trade, just as long as you're trading. Unfortunately that's human nature.

To be honest you don't even need a full-service broker. Open a discount brokerage account and make your own investment decisions. You'll save a significant amount on trading commissions and you'll most likely do much better making your own decisions than leaving them in the hands of a salesman who doesn't have your best interests at heart.

But what about the analysts? Why can't you take their recommendations at face value? The problem is the system is flawed. Honest analysts don't make it big in the industry, so the successful ones you hear about are, in all probability, not super-honest.

They have absolutely no incentive to actually perform an objective analysis because they're not rewarded for their analytical skills, but rewarded commensurate with their ability to generate corporate business and trading activity.

Their loyalty is to the company they work for, the company that pays their salary and the company that gives them fat bonuses at the end of each year. Their loyalty is not to you but to the brokerages.

Think about it. If you were paid to sell cars that weren't particularly good, would you tell potential purchasers about the problems with the cars you sell and suggest they go to your competitor to buy a better one?

Or would you try to maximize your income by selling your cars?

If you selected the former choice, then you wouldn't be in that industry very long.

Now pretend you're an analyst.

If your remuneration was tightly coupled to making a client's stock price go up, would you tell people about another company, who isn't your client, but whose stock is better than the one you're hawking? Or would you issue a strong buy recommendation on your stock so more people would purchase it and the price would move up?

You can answer that at your leisure. However it should be painfully obvious that nobody, especially not you, should take an analyst's recommendation at face value. Always do your own research and come to your own decision on what to buy or sell and when to do it.

And in case you still have doubts, here's a quote from Investors Business Daily.

"... from the late 1990's through 2001, fewer than 2% of brokers' stock recommendations were sells, according to Thomson First Call. That number is now closer to 10%, thanks in part to NASD rules that took effect in September. Still, it's a highly lopsided figure when **nearly three out of four stocks follow the general market trend.** Trusting analyst buy ratings is iffy even in a bull market. In a downtrend, it's a ticket to ruin."

That quote is saying that analysts were recommending you buy or hold 90% of the stocks being covered. Do you believe that 90% of the stocks being covered are a good buy? I hope not.

I'll leave this topic with a quote from Douglas Adams in his book, *Last Chance to See*. "Virtually everything we were told in Indonesia turned out not to be true, sometimes almost immediately. The only exception to this was when we were told that something would happen immediately, in which case it turned out not to be true over an extended period of time."

And speaking of things that turned out not to be true...

> *NEW YORK (Reuters) - HealthSouth Corp. fired Chief Executive and Chairman Richard Scrushy, saying on Monday it would grant no severance payments or benefits to the central figure in a widening probe into more than a billion dollars of possible accounting fraud.*
>
> *Federal securities regulators have accused HealthSouth and Scrushy of overstating earnings by $1.4 billion since 1999, and of inflating the value of assets by $800 million.*

Coincidentally I once worked for a consulting firm that did a significant piece of work for HealthSouth many years before their alleged fraud problems. We were a small team, culled from the firm's larger staff base, assembled to implement a powerful software system designed to allow HealthSouth to process information more efficiently.

This was a huge improvement and had the potential to save HealthSouth significant sums of money going forward. It was also a long-term project that could have included many phases.

To make a long story short, near the end of the initial phase, HealthSouth approached the team members and offered to hire them away from the consulting firm. Basically they raided the company and took the resources that had the knowledge of their newly developed system. While not technically illegal, it was unethical.

Needless to say, it left the consulting firm with a bad taste in its mouth. HealthSouth also established itself as a company that was willing to compromise its ethics in pursuit of the almighty dollar.

That simple action should have been enough for people to realize it was not a good place to work nor was it a good place in which to invest. Unfortunately, many people on the team were blinded by their increased salaries and stock options and ignored HealthSouth's unethical behaviour. They even purchased additional shares with their own money.

This was a classic case of short-term gain overriding good long-term common sense.

Small lapses in ethics usually lead to bigger lapses. It's a slippery slope that is often difficult to change once a company starts down that road.

Therefore it is imperative investors steer clear of any company that doesn't place significant importance on its ethics. If you hear of even seemingly small indiscretions, it's time to look elsewhere.

There are many other fish in the sea, and you certainly don't want, or for that matter need, to be stuck with an unethical one.

But even good, ethical companies can be bad investments. Let's venture back to the year 2000. Back then I was the editor of a Vancouver technology magazine. This was during the Bull market when Internet and technology stocks were propelling the market to absurd heights.

There were quite a few good companies around at the time and although they were over-valued, they just kept rising.

Whenever a small pullback occurred, people would consider it a buying opportunity and the stock would rise even further. Here's an editorial I wrote in an early 2000 issue.

The bulls are running in the streets. Not like they do in Pamplona, Spain, mind you, instead they represent a sustained rising stock market. Stocks have been advancing for over a decade, and show no sign of abating.

I think Superman best summed up this technology-fueled run when he said, "Up, Up, and Away." Some of the more optimistic among us cling to the words of another great hero, Buzz Lightyear, and join his shouts of, "To Infinity and Beyond."

Unfortunately the bulls won't last forever, they'll eventually tire. Then the bears will have some fun.

In the meantime, however, people from all walks of life are jumping on the stock market bandwagon. And why not? With a forgiving market and annual returns of over 100% within reach, what's not to like? In a market where a trained monkey can make money, smiles abound.

However it's a wise person who plans ahead. Knowing what to do before jumping on the bull can mean the difference between investing and gambling – wealth and bankruptcy, or at least making a few bucks and having to meet a margin call. The trick is to know how to manage your risk.

Rather than trying to make a quick profit, you should be looking to minimize your downside risk. The key concept, that bears repeating again and again, is the preservation of capital. No capital. No investment. No profit.

Of course in heady times such as these, it can be difficult to remember such concepts. So far, all downturns (or corrections) have resulted in a buying spree that serves to send stock prices right back up again. It wasn't always so in the past, and it won't always be so in the future.

Therefore it makes sense to assess yourself. Your strengths, your weaknesses, and your tolerance for pain – or risk as they like to say in the financial world. If your stock portfolio dropped 70% next week, and stayed down for the foreseeable future, how would it affect you? Would your lifestyle be affected significantly? Would you have trouble sleeping at night? Would you sell at a loss and vow never to invest in stocks again?

These questions will help you determine whether you're sufficiently diversified amongst the various asset classes (i.e. stocks, bonds, real estate, money market funds, etc.). Your answers will also tell you whether you should be in the stock market at all.

If you're still game, the next step is to formulate an investment plan. If you're in for the long haul, a "seat of the pants" strategy is not going to work. Granted, it may work in today's investment climate. But long term? Forget it.

Once you have a well thought out strategy (and you've objectively assessed yourself), stick with the plan – day in, day out. Be consistent and logical. And watch out for the dynamic duo of killer emotions: greed and fear.

Looking back, that editorial was strangely prescient.

When I wrote the bit about portfolios dropping 70%, I had no idea it would actually happen. I was trying to make a point and thought I'd overemphasize the downside. Unfortunately some people's portfolios did in fact drop 70% or more.

Those that held high-quality stocks (myself included) lost money. Those that held only speculative Internet stocks were wiped out.

The editorial illustrates a very important point.

Even excellent stocks can be driven to absurd pricing levels. When the markets reach silly heights, it's time to look elsewhere for your investments.

Perhaps the stock market will not be so sorely overpriced for another generation, but you should still be aware that you do not always have to be in the stock market.

Sometimes it's prudent to move your money to other types of non-equity investments.

But regardless of whether the markets are overvalued or not, you would do well to select stocks by following a time-tested and proven plan. And the best plan to follow is the one Warren Buffett himself uses. It consists of three basic steps:

1) Ask a series of questions to determine if a company is worth further investigation.

2) If so, determine the fundamental strength of the company.

3) If the company is fundamentally solid, determine what price to pay so there is a built-in margin of safety to maximize the probability of receiving market-beating returns.

The next chapters describe exactly how to implement each step in this plan.

ACTION PLAN

Learn how to use investment tools properly. Don't blindly follow systems or software no matter how professional the system looks or how much it's advertised or hyped in the media. Above all, understand what you're doing and think for yourself.

If you own actively managed mutual funds, find out exactly how much you're paying each year for the privilege. You'll probably find you're being charged too much. If so, take a serious look at Index funds and sector Exchange Traded Funds (ETFs). Investing properly with these types of funds will most likely provide you with returns superior to any actively managed funds you currently hold.

Consider closing any full-service brokerage accounts you might have and opening a discount brokerage account. Whether you do so or not, however, never blindly follow your broker's or any analyst's recommendations. Do your own research and due diligence before investing your money.

If you own a company that displays even the slightest hint of an integrity problem, no matter how small, get rid of it and replace it with one that doesn't.

Go through all of your investments and ask yourself why each one is in your portfolio. Is it because you're hoping to make a fortune overnight? If so, greed is probably clouding your judgment and you should liquidate your position in that stock.

On the flip side, when your research shows you're holding an excellent value stock but Wall Street, the media or others are telling anyone who'll listen it's out of favor, don't let fear coerce you into selling.

Chapter Ten
Picking Stocks

"Any fool can make things bigger and more complex... It takes a touch of
genius – and a lot of courage to move in the opposite direction."

Albert Einstein

S un. Surf. Sand. Ahhh, the laid back life at Cocoa Beach, Florida. There
are certainly worse ways to spend an afternoon than sitting in a
restaurant at the Cocoa Beach pier and watching the surfers below.

And interestingly enough, the surfers can teach you more than just how to
catch a wave. In fact they can teach you how to find good investments. To
see how, let's revisit a day I spent at Cocoa Beach.

As I sat in the Pier Restaurant, jutting out over the ocean high above the
surfers, I realized I had a unique perspective on how the surfing system
works. I watched one surfer as he used the system to near perfection. Since I
don't know his name, I'll call him "Dude."

Most of Dude's time was spent sitting on his board patiently waiting for a
good wave. When one appeared, he'd spin his board around, lie down on his
stomach and start paddling slowly with his hands. As the wave came up
behind him, he'd start paddling faster and kick furiously in an attempt to
catch the wave – after which he'd stand up and ride the wave in towards the
beach.

A few things struck me right away. First, surfers have to take advantage of
opportunity. No matter how hard they hope or wish, they can't make a wave
appear. Nor do they swim around the ocean seeking waves. They don't listen
to the radio announcing where the last big wave had recently been spotted
and then waste untold energy speeding to that spot only to find they'd missed
the proverbial boat. Rather they know that if they're patient, a good wave will
eventually come along.

Once a wave does appear, they need to decide whether it's a good one and
if so, immediately take the correct action. The wave doesn't care about the
surfers nor does it even know about them. It just continues on its merry way

without regard to who uses it or who misses it. But how do surfers know a good wave when they see it and what exactly does taking the correct action entail?

To answer that, let's go back to our surfer. Dude knows a good wave from experience. The size, shape and speed are all taken into consideration when making his determination. In essence, he looks at the fundamental attributes of a wave and applies specific formulas (albeit intuitively rather than explicitly) he's learned from experience to determine whether it's a good one or not.

Once he's happy with the wave, he takes the correct action. In Dude's case that means he has to work hard for a short period of time – when he's paddling and kicking furiously – in fact he goes all out, holding nothing back, in an attempt to catch the wave. He expends quite a bit of effort in this endeavor and initially he isn't moving too quickly.

However once he catches the wave, things became easier. Significantly easier. Dude's able to stop paddling and stand up on his board. No more paddling, no more kicking, just sun on his skin, wind in his hair and a terrific view of the approaching beach. And to top it all off, his speed increases rapidly.

In fact he goes much faster than he could possibly go by propelling himself using only his arms and legs – and get this, he's using much less energy than he did during his paddling phase. In essence Dude's going faster AND using less energy because he's harnessed the power of the wave for his purposes.

Of course he still has to make small course corrections along the way in order to ride the wave as long as possible and, perhaps, avoid other surfers. But all-in-all, once he's riding the wave, things are mostly automatic. And fun too!

Other, less skilled, surfers might not catch a good wave for a variety of reasons, including not recognizing when a good wave is coming, ignoring it or expending their efforts on less deserving waves.

But not Dude.

He consistently let lesser waves go by while others wasted effort and energy on them. But when he saw a good one, he was always ready to take the correct action and reap the rewards of a joyful ride to the beach. Often while others were too tired, not in position or simply not prepared to join him.

So how does Dude and his waves benefit your investments? In more ways than one as you shall see.

First, recognize that the market doesn't care about you, it doesn't even know about you and you cannot affect it. You can't hope or wish the market into doing what you want. It just continues on its merry way without regard to who uses the opportunities it presents or who misses them. In that respect the market is like a force of nature. It's not wrong, it's not right, it just IS. To be successful you need to hitch a ride on the market's coattails.

That means you shouldn't pick a stock with which you've fallen in love and hope the market will concur with your decision. Rather look at what the market gives you and pick only the very best of the best, stocks that have strong value given their current price.

Have patience. Don't force yourself to buy stocks just because everyone else is buying. Same with selling. Wait for the absolute best moment, the most opportune time, the time when logic should have you salivating about the potential and then go for it in a big way. Swing for the fences. Stand up on your surfboard and catch that wave!

Others might not join you because they're busy following the crowd, they're distracted following lesser offerings or they're just not prepared – perhaps they're in debt up the yin-yang and although they see the opportunity, they can't grab it. This would be similar to a surfer seeing the perfect wave but being out of position, because he just caught a lesser wave and is standing near the beach, or not having his board with him because he wasn't prepared.

Furthermore, don't wander around aimlessly chasing the latest hot investment. This means you don't buy the stock that just went up 200% simply because it went up 200% or the media is hyping it. Wait for the good investment opportunities to come to you. Don't waste your efforts on less than stellar "opportunities," prefer instead to let them pass you by.

Next, learn to recognize a good investment opportunity. This is where you have to initially work hard for a short period of time (of course with the advent of computers and the Internet, you don't have to work as hard as those who came before you).

So how do you recognize a good investment?

Whereas Dude used his experience to determine a good wave, when it comes to investing, it's better to quantify the important concepts as much as possible. To start this quantification effort, we'll first look at seven important questions to ask *before* investing in a company's stock and then we'll see what Benjamin Graham, the father of value investing, has to say. First the questions.

1) Is the company free to adjust prices to inflation?

2) Is it likely that a new product or service will come along within the next 10 years and completely wipe out customers' needs for this product or service?

3) Does the company have a strong moat? A moat is one or more of brand, exclusivity, size or price (for example, does the company have a strong, trusted and recognizable brand, does it have an identifiable consumer monopoly in its region or globally, is it large enough to overcome competitors or can it compete effectively on price for long periods of time?).

4) What does the company do or have that protects it from competition and keeps its customers coming back?

5) If a new competitor came along with one year's worth of unlimited funds to fight for the company's customers, how vulnerable would the company's future be?

6) If the company had to quit advertising or expanding for the next year, how badly would it be hurt? Could it recover after that year and bring customers back?

7) Does the company produce a product or service that has been used by its customers for at least the past 10 years? Will this company's products be used for the next 10 years?

If the company you're looking at can make it past these questions, chances are you're looking at a great company that just might make a terrific investment.

On the other hand, if the company fails to pass through these questions, it's probably best for you to ignore it and move on.

Once you've completed the questions, the next step is to listen to what Benjamin Graham said in his book, "The Intelligent Investor." In that book he laid out some criteria for a good value stock – which is most likely to lead to a good investment. He states that it should have:

1. An Earnings/Price (inverse of P/E) that is double the AAA bond yield.
2. A P/E that is 40% of the highest annual average P/E ratio achieved by the stock in the most recent five years. (average P/E is Average Price for the year / Earnings for the year).
3. A dividend yield of 2/3 the AAA bond yield.
4. Total debt that is less than tangible book value.
5. A Current Ratio of two or more. The Current Ratio is Current Assets divided by Current Liabilities. This is an indication of a company's ability to pay its debt from its income.
6. A price less than two-thirds the Net Current Asset Value, which is calculated as Current Assets minus Total Liabilities.
7. Total debt at or less than the net quick liquidation value.
8. Earnings that have doubled in the most recent ten years.
9. No more than two declines in earnings of 5% or more in the past 10 years.

Points 1 to 3 measure risk, 4 and 7 measure financial soundness and 8 and 9 show a history of stable earnings. Of course not all types of stocks will lend themselves to all of the points Graham listed (for instance, some stocks don't pay dividends), so you might choose to ignore or modify some of Graham's suggestions. If you do this, however, be sure you know why you're doing it and how it affects the stock's risk and soundness.

Graham also wrote, "liabilities are real but the assets are of questionable value." Graham believed that not all assets were of equal quality. Rather, some were significantly better than others. He estimated the differences between asset classes by associating a percentage of real value with each asset class. In his mind, cash is worth 100% of its value, Receivables are worth 75 to 90%, Inventories are 50 to 75% and fixed assets are worth 1 to 50%.

Richard Sloan, a professor at the University of Michigan, applied this thinking to earnings. In essence he states that not all types of earnings are of equal quality. At the top of the heap, as with assets, is the cash component. Non-cash earnings, such as revenues that aren't yet realized as cash or those based on accounting assumptions, are of lower quality. As an example, revenues counted when goods or services are sold, but before the cash is collected, is of a lower quality than revenues backed up with cash in the bank.

Sloan represents this idea using the "Accruals Ratio" which is simply a company's Total Accruals divided by its Total Assets.

Total Accruals can be approximated using a company's *Net Income* minus its *Cash Flow from Continuing Operations* minus its *Cash Flow from Investing*. Putting it all together, we can write the formula as:

```
Accruals Ratio = (Net Income - Cash Flow from
Continuing Operations - Cash Flow from Investing) /
                  Total Assets
```

Net Income can be found on a company's Income Statement, Total Assets can be found on its Balance Sheet and the cash flows can be found on its Cash Flow Statement.

The lower the Accruals Ratio, the better. Sloan further classifies anything below negative 5% as a good buy, anything above 5% as a bad buy (or a sell if you currently own it) and anything in between as neutral.

Let's look at an example. If you view Oracle Corporation's (ticker ORCL) annual financial statements for the year ended May 2003, you'll see the following:

```
1. Net Income was $2,307 million.
2. Cash Flow from Continuing Operations was 3,023
   million.
3. Cash Flow from Investing was 895 million.
4. Total Assets were 11,064 million.
```

After doing the math you'll arrive at an Accruals Ratio of negative 14.56%. Since this is well below Sloan's cutoff of negative 5%, ORCL would pass this test, with flying colours, and you could go on to research it further to see if it really is a good investment.

One word of caution, the Accruals Ratio doesn't work for financial type companies as their cash flows are more complicated to analyze.

The Accruals Ratio is one filter you can use. However you should never rely on just one filter to make your investment decisions. There are many interconnected things you need to look at before you invest your hard earned money and it's up to you to perform your own due diligence and be comfortable with the stocks you pick.

Ultimately you need to take responsibility for your investment decisions but a good place to start is with a company's financial statements. Specifically you should scrutinize the Income Statement (also called the Statement of Earnings), the Balance Sheet (also called the Statement of Financial Condition) and the Statement of Cash Flows.

The Income Statement shows how the company operated in order to generate revenue, what expenses it incurred and any profits (or losses) it made during a specific period.

The Balance Sheet shows what assets a company owns as well as what it owes creditors and shareholders. It is a snapshot of the company at a specific date.

The Statement of Cash Flows provides information about how cash was generated and where it was used during a specific period.

You can find these statements online or in the company's annual report. Once you have them, however, you need to know what the numbers mean. As a primer, I'll point out some of the relevant data at which you should be looking. I'll start with the Income Statement.

The first thing to realize is that under today's accounting rules, companies can make their earnings look much better than they are in reality. And it's all quite legal. Therefore the onus is on you, the investor, to filter through the garbage and find the true picture. You should never accept at face value the rosy picture described in a company's annual report, nor should you feel any better because an auditor has given a company's report its blessing. As I mentioned earlier, companies can (and most certainly do) legally dress up their results to look much better than reality.

Take earnings for instance. The accounting rules allow a company to record revenues when a sale is made rather than when cash is deposited into its account. Similarly expenses are recorded when they are processed rather than when the actual cash is paid out. If you realize that Earnings is the difference between Sales and Expenses, you'll quickly see that a company's management has considerable leeway in manipulating earnings for a specific period.

For example, a company can sell their products and give their customers a year to pay. Although they won't receive the cash for a year, they're able to record their sales immediately. This practice can boost their current quarterly revenues, however there's no actual cash backing it up in that quarter. Keep that in mind when you look at earnings.

Getting into the Income Statement specifics, the first thing you'll see is the sales figure that shows how much was made from selling products and services. Higher sales aren't necessarily better if those sales aren't translated into more money in the bank.

Car companies are a good example of this as they sometimes boost their sales figures without a corresponding boost in profits. They do this by discounting their cars, offering incentives and extending credit to people with less than stellar credit ratings – who end up declaring bankruptcy and not paying for their cars.

The effect is that while the company is increasing, sales it's not necessarily increasing the actual cash it can deposit into its bank account. Think of it this way, you can make a great deal of sales selling dollar bills for 80 cents, but you'll always come out with a loss at the end of the day.

On the expense side, of the Income Statement, the first deduction you'll see is the Cost of Goods Sold. This is the amount of money it took to make the sales. There are also other expenses, such as administrative, depreciation and Research and Development costs.

The difference between Sales and Cost of Goods Sold is the Gross Profit. Here is the calculation.

$$\texttt{Gross Profit = Sales - Cost of Goods Sold}$$

If a company has been selling dollar bills for 80 cents, the problem will show up here.

The gross profit margin is given by the following formula.

$$\texttt{Gross Profit Margin = Gross Profit / Sales}$$

This measures how much money a company keeps after paying for the cost of goods it sold. An increasing Gross Profit Margin, over the years, is a good sign while a decreasing one should raise a flag and means you need to delve deeper into the company's financials.

After Depreciation and Amortization as well as other operating expenses are subtracted we arrive at the company's Earnings from Operations (also called EBIT). This value describes how successful the company was in its ongoing business operations. You can calculate the Operating Profit Margin as follows.

$$\texttt{Operating Profit Margin = Earnings from Operations / Sales}$$

A rising value, over the years, is better but it still doesn't tell the entire story. A company can increase this value in the short term using a variety of creative accounting techniques, so you should never base your decisions on just this number (in fact you should never base your investment decisions on any one number. To view a company's financial health requires you to look at a variety of relevant measures taken together).

After taking into account non-operating income and subtracting non-operating expenses, such as interest paid and taxes, we arrive at the Net Earnings figure.

This is the bottom line and is what the company reports when its earnings are released.

The calculation for the Net Profit Margin is shown below.

Net Profit Margin = Net Earnings / Sales

This value shows the percentage of profit earned for each dollar of sales. Of all the values we've seen so far, Net Profit and Net Profit Margin are the most illuminating and this is where you should start your analysis. Keep in mind that, in addition to trend, a company's margins should be compared to other companies in the same industry. Comparing margins of companies in different industries rarely provides useful information.

After you've inspected the Income Statement, it's time to turn your attention to the Balance Sheet. Keep in mind that all of a company's financial statements are intertwined. You need to view them all together rather than evaluating one or two in isolation.

When a company makes a sale, the Income Statement is affected because the Sales value increases. However the Balance Sheet is also affected because a corresponding increase is added to the Cash (or Receivables) line. Inventory is reduced appropriately and the Cost of Goods Sold (back on the Income Statement) is increased. Profits or losses result in a change of equity on the Balance Sheet and any cash shows up on the Statement of Cash Flows.

As you can see, you need a basic understanding of all the statements in order to properly analyze a company's financial health.

But back to the Balance Sheet. This statement summarizes the company's assets and its liabilities (both to outsiders and its shareholders). The calculation is shown below.

Assets = Liabilities + Shareholder's Equity

Current Assets describe how much cash a company has and includes cash on hand, cash equivalents and other liquid assets that can be converted into cash in a relatively short period of time. Short term investments (Marketable Securities), Inventories and Accounts Receivables are also included under Current Assets.

The Balance Sheet also contains long-term assets such as properties, equipment required to carry on business and other fixed assets. There are also other types of assets such as Goodwill, long-term receivables and deferred income tax charges.

The important line to look at is the Total Assets figure.

On the Liabilities side, the Balance Sheet records Current Liabilities (which are expected to be paid within a year and include Accounts Payable, Dividends Payable and short-term loans and Taxes).

Other Liabilities contains entries that are expected to take longer to pay off, such as Long-term loans and deferred income tax credits. The important line, for liabilities, is the Total Liabilities figure.

The final section on the Balance Sheet is the Shareholders' Equity portion. This describes the ownership interests in the company or the value of the company that would be available for splitting between the owners if the company was liquidated and all liabilities were paid using its assets.

One important line in the Shareholders' Equity section is the Retained Earnings value. It represents earnings, since the company began its operations, that have not been distributed to shareholders but reinvested into the company.

The final statement we'll look at is the Statement of Cash Flows. In the past, this statement had often been ignored in favor of the Income Statement and Balance Sheet. However the Cash Flows statement can provide an important view into a company's financial health.

It shows how cash has flowed both into and out of a company during a specific period.

The main entries to look for are the Cash Flow from Continuing Operations, Cash Flow from Investing Activities and Cash Flow from Financing Activities.

As I mentioned above, we can use the first two entries to estimate the total accruals when calculating Richard Sloan's Accrual Ratio.

Cash Flow from Continuing Operations contains information about the production and delivery of goods and services. It shows the amount of actual cash that has been generated from a company's internal operations. If a company cannot generate enough cash internally in order to carry on business, it will raise the cash through external sources (such as borrowing or selling additional shares).

Cash Flow from Investing Activities includes the purchase or sale of non-cash equivalent securities and capital equipment. It also includes interest received for loans and other lending activities.

Cash Flow from Financing Activities includes funds borrowed and loan principal repayments among other things.

More than any other statement, this one provides a look at how much actual cash a company is generating. It is much more difficult for a company to play around with cash figures since they represent actual cash in the bank and are thus harder to legally manipulate.

Free Cash Flow is another useful measure you should look at because it takes into account the need for cash to support investment in new capital in addition to maintaining current operations. You can calculate Free Cash Flow (FCF) as follows.

FCF = Cash Flow from Continuing Operations – Capital Expenditures

You've already seen the Cash Flow from Continuing Operations value. The Capital Expenditures value can be found in the Cash Flow from Investing Activities section (usually it's the first line) and can also be called *Payments for plant, rental machines and other property* or something similar.

Now that you have a basic understanding of the financial statements, let's turn our attention to analyzing them.

Fundamental Analysis involves looking at a company's historical financial condition and using it to evaluate the probability the company's value will increase or decrease in the future. Combined with the company's current share price you can then make a decision on whether to purchase or sell shares.

One way to analyze a company's fundamentals is to look at some of the key financial ratios. These ratios can give you a snapshot of how a company is doing. However it is important to use these ratios in the proper context, such as comparing them with previous years' ratios and against other companies in the same industry.

Two companies that have similar ratios at a specific point in time can be moving in completely opposite directions. Therefore it's vital you look at the trend rather than simply relying on an isolated snapshot.

So what are some key financial ratios? I've already mentioned a few from Benjamin Graham's book, "The Intelligent Investor." But let's expand on those and discuss the interpretation.

There are three important groups: Liquidity ratios, Leverage ratios and Profitability ratios. I'll start with Liquidity ratios.

The Current Ratio can be used to measure the ability of a company to meet its short-term debts. The calculation is shown below.

```
Current Ratio = Current Assets / Current Liabilities
```

The higher the value, the better. Values below one indicate the company cannot cover its current liabilities using its current assets. The Current Ratio is also limited in that some of the components of the Current Assets are not necessarily liquid (recall that Current Assets include Accounts Receivables and Inventories which might not be readily converted into cash at their stated values).

A better ratio is the Quick Ratio. It is calculated as follows.

```
Quick Ratio = (Current Assets - Inventory) / Current
                        Liabilities
```

Since Inventory is considered one of the least liquid components of Current Assets, it is removed before dividing by the Current Liabilities. This gives a better view of the company's ability to meet its short-term obligations.

Another way of measuring short-term ability to meet debts is the Cash Flow Liquidity Ratio. The formula is shown below.

```
Cash Flow Liquidity Ratio = (Cash + Marketable
Securities + Cash Flow from Continuing Operations) /
                  Current Liabilities
```

This ratio shows the amount of actual cash available compared to short-term liabilities.

You can compare all three ratios to help determine a company's ability to meet its short-term obligations. If they are moving in different directions you should dig deeper to determine the reason. At the end of the day a company needs to generate sufficient cash to meet its obligations and continue operations. If it can't do this because it cannot, say, collect on its accounts receivables or it has to sell its old inventory at a substantial discount, then it will ultimately have to borrow money and take on debt.

Leverage ratios are the second important group because they describe how much debt a company has and its ability to handle it. Three important ones are described below.

The Debt Ratio is defined as:

```
Debt Ratio = Total Liabilities / Total Assets
```

The Long-term Debt to Total Capitalization's formula is:

```
Long term Debt / (Long term Debt + Shareholders'
                  Equity)
```

The Debt to Equity ratio is calculated as follows.

```
Debt to Equity Ratio = Total Liabilities /
          Shareholders' Equity
```

These ratios measure how much debt the company is using to finance its operations.

Companies that have too much debt are exposed to interest rate fluctuations as well as needing to pay down principal balances at some point in the future. Therefore cash used to do this is not available for other purposes. Additionally, companies might find it difficult to obtain further financing if they are too highly leveraged.

Of course not all debt is bad, but significant debt should raise flags indicating you need to do more research into how the debt was acquired and what it was used for.

Another important debt measurement ratio is Cash-to-debt. It is defined as follows.

```
Cash to Debt Ratio = (Cash and Equivalents + Marketable
     Securities) / (Short term debt + Long term debt)
```

All values can be found on the Balance Sheet. This ratio tells you how much cash a company has relative to its debt. Higher values are better. Values below 1 should raise a flag indicating a potential debt overload problem.

A ratio that measures how well a company can service its debt is Times Interest Earned. It's calculated as:

$$\text{Times Interest Earned Ratio} = \text{Operating Profit} / \text{Interest Expense}$$

The higher the number the better, but if the Operating Profit is not a result of real cash, this ratio can mislead you. To get a better feel for how well a company can service its debt with the cash it is generating, you can use the Cash Interest Coverage ratio. The calculation is:

$$\text{Cash Interest Coverage Ratio} = (\text{Cash Flow from Operations} + \text{Interest Paid} + \text{Taxes Paid}) / \text{Interest Paid}$$

These ratios will give you an idea of how well a company is positioned to meet its interest payments.

The final group of ratios are those pertaining to Profitability. I've already talked about Gross Profit Margin, Operating Profit Margin and Net Profit Margin, so I'll now introduce Cash Flow Margin. It's calculated as:

$$\text{Cash Flow Margin} = \text{Cash Flow from Continuing Operations} / \text{Net Sales}$$

When all is said and done, cash is what really matters. Cash is how companies pay dividends, service debt, invest in new equipment and provide for Research and Development. Therefore it's useful to see how much actual cash is being generated from sales. If sales are high, but real cash from operations is low, then you need to know why. Is it because the company is selling dollar bills for 80 cents? Are they using some creative accounting tricks? Do they have too much debt? Whatever the reason, you need to know before investing your money.

Two other useful profitability measures are Return on Investment (ROI) and Return on Equity (ROE). They're calculated as follows:

$$\text{ROI} = \text{Net Profit} / \text{Total Assets}$$

```
ROE = Net Profit / Shareholders' Equity
```

They measure how well the company is managing its investments in assets and how well its doing in creating returns for shareholders respectively.

The final ratio I'll mention is Cash Return on Assets. It's calculated as:

```
Cash Return on Assets Ratio = Cash Flow from Continuing
                Operations / Total Assets
```

It's useful when compared to Return on Investment because it shows how much actual cash is being generated in relation to assets. If ROI and Cash Return on Assets are moving in different directions or at significantly different rates, it indicates a possible problem that you should look into.

Relative Sales growth is also important. Comparing Sales growth to Inventory and Accounts Receivables growth can be illuminating.

If Inventory is growing at a faster rate than Sales, that might mean the company can't sell its products fast enough. And in most cases, the inventory will be worth less as time passes.

To use this measure, calculate Sales growth for two periods by dividing the value for the most recent period's date by the value for the previous period's date.

So if Sales in 2003 was $42,635 million and in 2002 it was $36,360 million, then Sales growth would be:

```
(42,635 million / 36,360 million) - 1 = 17.4%
```

(Note that a good rule of thumb is for Sales growth to be above 10% per year.)

Perform a similar calculation for the Inventory values. If Inventory at the end of 2003 was $2,942 million and it was $3,148 million at the end of 2002, then Inventory growth would be:

```
(2,942 million / 3,148 million) - 1 = -6.5%
```

In the example, Sales growth is significantly higher than Inventory growth (which has in fact decreased) – a good sign. Ideally you want your potential investments to grow sales at a much higher rate than inventories are growing.

Of course some companies (such as Service companies) don't have significant inventories, so Inventory to Sales is not relevant for all industries.

You can analyze Sales to Accounts Receivables growth in a similar manner. Calculate the Accounts Receivables growth as above and compare it with Sales growth. So if Accounts Receivables were $10,026 million in 2003 and $9,915 million in 2002, then growth would be:

```
(10,026 million / 9,915 million) - 1 = 1.1%
```

Since the resulting figure is well below the 17.4% Sales growth we calculated above, there are no concerns with this example.

However if Accounts Receivables growth starts to get ahead of Sales growth you should dig deeper to determine the cause. It could mean the company is having difficulty collecting what it's owed and that could mean it will lose money to bad debts. Since it's already booked the revenue associated with the receivables, it won't have the underlying cash in the bank to support those revenue numbers. That's bad news.

If both Accounts Receivables growth and Inventory growth start to outpace Sales growth, then you should definitely start to worry. Don't invest in such companies until you can determine why this is happening (or better yet, move onto another candidate).

Taken together, these ratios, trends and relations can illuminate potential problems with a company. Remember, it's imperative you look at these data together rather than in isolation. A company that has stellar sales figures might not be a good investment if it's not generating any cash flow. Similarly a company with lower sales might be a cash cow with no debt and an exceptional future. Never base your investment decisions on just a piece of the picture. Ensure you're looking at the entire thing.

Before we continue, it's important to note that what I've covered so far doesn't tell you everything. There's valuable information the key ratios won't reveal.

One example is how well a company's industry will perform in the future. When automobiles were becoming popular in the late 1800s, horse carriage manufacturers were facing dismal prospects. It didn't matter whether their financial ratios were excellent or their businesses had a long history of generating profits, the fact their industry was about to be wiped out by the "horseless carriage" was not something fundamental analysis could tell you.

Rather you had to be able to see the societal trend of moving away from horses and towards the internal combustion engine for power. If you missed it, your investments would have suffered. That's an important lesson. Although financial ratios are crucial in helping you determine a company's health, they cannot be solely relied upon. You need to look at other factors as well.

That being said, however, the **Pragmatic Investor**'s Fundamental Analyzer function can give you a head start by automating some of the basics.

It uses a number of time-tested heuristic filters developed by super-investors such as Warren Buffett and Benjamin Graham to find companies that are worthy of further consideration. Note you don't have to use the software to evaluate a stock because you can manually calculate its rating using the steps below.

However you'll most likely notice that the process is very repetitive, error-prone and calculation intensive. Of course if you're using the software, it just takes a few mouse clicks.

With that out of the way, let's dive in and look at the important numbers and also take a look at what to do with those numbers. There are 11 filters and each filter is given a rating of Excellent, Very Good, Good, Marginal or Bad. Here are the filters:

1. If **Return On Equity (ROE)** is greater than or equal to 30% then rate Excellent; If ROE is greater than 20% and less than or equal to 30% then rate Very Good; If ROE greater than 15% and less than or equal to 20% then rate Good; If ROE is greater than 12% and less than or equal to 15% then rate Marginal. Otherwise, rate Bad.

2. The more times **Net Income** has grown in the past 5 years, the better. Rate Excellent if it has grown 4 times, Very Good if it has grown 3 times, Good if it has grown 2 times, Marginal if it has grown 1 time or bad if it has not grown at all in the past 5 years.

3. The more times **Cash Flow** has grown in the past 5 years, the better. Determine the rating in the same manner as for Net Income.

4. If **EPS / Long-term AAA Bond Yield** is less than the stock's current share price, then rate Excellent; otherwise rate Bad.

5. If the company's current **Profit Margin** is greater than the company's average industry Profit Margin, then rate Excellent; if it's equal, rate Good. Otherwise rate Bad.

6. If the company's current **Profit Margin** is greater than its 5-year average, then rate Excellent.

7. If the company's current **Long-term Debt / Net Income** is less than 5 then rate Excellent; if it's between 5 and 16 then rate Good. Otherwise rate Bad.

8. If the company's **Gross Profit Margin** is greater than or equal to 40% then rate Excellent; if it's between 20% and 40% then rate Good; otherwise rate Bad.

9. The more times **Net Earnings** has grown in the past 5 years, the better. Determine the rating in the same manner as for Net Income.

10. If the company's **Net Earnings Margin** is greater than or equal to 20% then rate Excellent; if it's between 10% and 20% then rate Good; otherwise rate Bad.

11. If the company has been buying back its shares in each of the past 5 years (**Issuance (Retirement) of Stock, Net**) and it has increased these buybacks in each of the past 5 years, then rate Excellent. If it has been buying back its shares, but not increasing the amount in each of the past 5 years, then rate Good. Otherwise rate Bad.

Once you have a rating for each filter, assign a score to each rating as follows: Excellent = 4, Very Good = 3, Good = 2, Marginal = 1 and Bad = 0.

Then add up the scores and divide by 11. This will give you the average overall rating for the company.

For example, if the stock we are evaluating rates Excellent for filter (1), Good for (2), Very Good for (3), Bad for (4), Good for (5), Good for (6), Excellent for (7), Good for (8), Marginal for (9), Good for (10) and Bad for (11), then our total score would be 4 + 2 + 3 + 0 + 2 + 2 + 4 + 2 + 1 + 2 + 0 = 22.

We would then divide the total score by 11 (i.e. 22 / 11) to get a rating of 2.

Going back to our ratings scale, we see a rating of 2 equates to Good. So from a fundamentals perspective, our stock would be rated as Good. Note you should generally only consider stocks that are rated Very Good or Excellent.

Once you've selected potential investments using the Fundamental Analyzer or by manually following the steps described above, you should further research your selections as described earlier in this chapter.

Then when you've worked through the basics and are happy with the fundamental results, the final piece is to determine the company's **Moat Strength**.

Earlier in this chapter you learned the 7 important questions to ask. Question 3 dealt with a company's moat. According to Warren Buffett a moat protects a company from competitors. The stronger the moat, the harder it is for a competitor to hurt the company by stealing its customers.

If you answered question 3, you should have a good idea of how strong your company's moat is, however it is necessary to back up that answer with some quantitative results.

With that in mind, we can use **Pat Dorsey's** (he's Morningstar's Director of Stock Analysis) research to determine if a company's moat is strong. Dorsey uses 4 elements that, taken together, do a relatively good job of showing which companies have strong economic moats.

In fact he states, "The concept of economic moats is crucial to the way Morningstar analyzes stocks because a moat is the characteristic that helps great-performing companies to stay that way."

He goes on to credit Warren Buffett and Harvard professor Michael Porter for the idea of an economic moat. In fact Buffett adds a fifth element, to Dorsey's four, for determining moat strength.

Here are Dorsey and Buffett's 5 Moat defining criteria:

1. **Free Cash Flow / Sales** is 5 percent or better (you should go back 5 years and require that the company beat this mark in all 5 years). Give the company 1 point if it passes or 0 points if it doesn't.

2. **Net Margins** (Net Income / Sales) greater than 15 percent (again, the company should beat this mark in each of the past 5 years). Give the company 1 point if it passes or 0 points if it doesn't.

3. **Return on Equity** above 15 percent (in each of the past 5 years). Give the company 1 point if it passes or 0 points if it doesn't.

4. **Return on Assets** (Net Income / Total Assets) higher than 6 percent in each of the past 5 years. Give the company 1 point if it passes or 0 points if it doesn't.
5. Buffett also likes to use **Depreciation / Gross Profit** being less than 18% for a general pass and 8% or less for an A+. He's found that companies with lower Depreciation tend to have a sustained durable competitive advantage (which translates into a strong economic moat). Give the company 2 points if it passes with 8% or less, 1 point if it is between 8% and 18% and 0 points if it is 18% or higher.

Then add up the final score to determine the company's Moat strength. Moats are rated on a 6-point scale. Moat Strengths of 5 or 6 are considered excellent, a Moat Strength of 4 is considered good and Moat Strengths below 4 are considered weak.

You should ensure that quantitative result you just calculated agrees with your answer to question 3 of the 7 important questions we looked at earlier. If it doesn't, you need to determine why.

At this point we've discussed all the important pieces for determining whether a company is fundamentally sound. Since calculating the fundamentals rating and the moat strength are straightforward, I'll leave that as an exercise for you to work through on your own. Simply select a stock, go to either Yahoo! Finance or Microsoft's Money Central to find the relevant data and follow the steps I've outlined above.

However the analysis I discussed at the beginning of this chapter might be a little less straightforward, so let's look at an example using Oracle Corp. (ticker ORCL). Oracle scored high on the fundamental analyzer and also has a strong moat, so we can consider it as a potential investment candidate and analyze it further.

As I mentioned before, further analysis begins by scrutinizing the three important financial statements.

I've listed them below.

Statement 1 shows ORCL's Income statements for the 5 years ended 2003.

Financial data in U.S. dollars

Annual Income Statement (Values in Millions)	5/2003	5/2002	5/2001	5/2000	5/1999
Sales	9,475.0	9,673.0	10,859.7	10,130.1	8,827.3
Cost of Sales	2,015.0	2,043.0	2,449.1	2,551.8	2,688.8
Gross Operating Profit	7,460.0	7,630.0	8,410.6	7,578.3	6,138.5
Selling, General & Admin. Expense	3,693.0	3,696.0	4,286.6	4,107.3	3,890.2
Other Taxes	0.0	0.0	0.0	0.0	0.0
EBITDA	3,767.0	3,934.0	4,124.0	3,471.0	2,248.3
Depreciation & Amortization	327.0	363.0	346.9	390.9	375.4
EBIT	3,440.0	3,571.0	3,777.1	3,080.1	1,872.9
Other Income, Net	1.0	-143.0	218.2	7,062.2	130.6
Total Income Avail for Interest Exp.	3,441.0	3,428.0	3,995.3	10,142.3	2,003.5
Interest Expense	16.0	20.0	24.0	18.9	21.4
Minority Interest	0.0	0.0	0.0	0.0	0.0
Pre-tax Income	3,425.0	3,408.0	3,971.3	10,123.4	1,982.1
Income Taxes	1,118.0	1,184.0	1,410.1	3,826.6	692.3
Special Income/Charges	0.0	0.0	0.0	0.0	0.0
Net Income from Cont. Operations	2,307.0	2,224.0	2,561.1	6,296.8	1,289.8
Net Income from Discont. Opers.	0.0	0.0	0.0	0.0	0.0
Net Income from Total Operations	2,307.0	2,224.0	2,561.1	6,296.8	1,289.8
Normalized Income	2,307.0	2,224.0	2,561.1	6,296.8	1,289.8
Extraordinary Income	0.0	0.0	0.0	0.0	0.0
Income from Cum. Eff. of Acct. Chg.	0.0	0.0	0.0	0.0	0.0
Income from Tax Loss Carryforward	0.0	0.0	0.0	0.0	0.0
Other Gains (Losses)	0.0	0.0	0.0	0.0	0.0
Total Net Income	**2,307.0**	**2,224.0**	**2,561.1**	**6,296.8**	**1,289.8**
Dividends Paid per Share	0.00	0.00	0.00	0.00	0.00
Preferred Dividends	0.00	0.00	0.00	0.00	0.00

Statement 1

The Pragmatic Investor

Statement 2 shows ORCL's Balance Sheet.

Financial data in U.S. dollars

Annual Balance Sheet (Values in Millions)	5/2003	5/2002	5/2001	5/2000	5/1999
Assets					
Current Assets					
Cash and Equivalents	4,737.0	3,095.0	4,449.2	7,429.2	1,785.7
Receivables	2,221.0	2,329.0	2,713.9	2,790.2	2,479.0
Inventories	0.0	0.0	0.0	0.0	0.0
Other Current Assets	2,269.0	3,304.0	1,800.1	664.0	1,182.5
Total Current Assets	9,227.0	8,728.0	8,963.2	10,883.3	5,447.3
Non-Current Assets					
Property, Plant & Equipment, Gross	2,556.0	2,337.0	2,303.7	2,125.1	2,023.5
Accum. Depreciation & Depletion	1,494.0	1,350.0	1,328.9	1,190.6	1,036.0
Property, Plant & Equipment, Net	1,062.0	987.0	974.8	934.5	987.5
Intangibles	345.0	446.0	716.2	1,149.0	476.5
Other Non-Current Assets	430.0	639.0	376.0	110.0	348.4
Total Non-Current Assets	1,837.0	2,072.0	2,067.0	2,193.5	1,812.4
Total Assets	**11,064.0**	**10,800.0**	**11,030.2**	**13,076.8**	**7,259.7**
Liabilities & Shareholder's Equity					
Current Liabilities					
Accounts Payable	228.0	228.0	270.1	287.5	283.9
Short Term Debt	153.0	0.0	2.8	2.7	3.6
Other Current Liabilities	3,777.0	3,732.0	3,643.6	5,572.1	2,758.8
Total Current Liabilities	4,158.0	3,960.0	3,916.6	5,862.2	3,046.4
Non-Current liabilites					
Long Term Debt	175.0	298.0	300.8	300.8	304.1
Deferred Income Taxes	186.0	204.0	327.8	266.1	135.9
Other Non-Current Liabilities	225.0	221.0	207.1	186.2	77.9
Minority Interest	0.0	0.0	0.0	0.0	0.0
Total Non-Current Liabilities	586.0	723.0	835.7	753.1	517.9
Total Liabilities	**4,744.0**	**4,683.0**	**4,752.2**	**6,615.4**	**3,564.2**
Shareholder's Equity					
Preferred Stock Equity	0.0	0.0	0.0	0.0	0.0
Common Stock Equity	6,320.0	6,117.0	6,277.8	6,461.5	3,695.3
Total Equity	6,320.0	6,117.0	6,277.8	6,461.5	3,695.3
Total Liabilities & Stock Equity	**11,064.0**	**10,800.0**	**11,030.0**	**13,076.9**	**7,259.5**
Total Common Shares Outstanding	5.2 Bil	5.4 Bil	5.6 Bil	5.6 Bil	5.7 Bil

Statement 2

Statement 3 shows ORCL's Statement of Cash Flows.

Financial data in U.S. dollars

Annual Cash Flow (in Millions)	5/2003	5/2002	5/2001	5/2000	5/1999
Cash Flow from Operating Activities					
Net Income (Loss)	2,307.0	2,224.0	2,561.1	6,296.8	1,289.8
Depreciation and Amortization	327.0	363.0	346.9	390.9	375.4
Deferred Income Taxes	90.0	0.0	18.0	-16.7	20.4
Operating (Gains) Losses	239.0	439.0	272.7	-6,801.6	72.5
Extraordinary (Gains) Losses	0.0	0.0	0.0	0.0	0.0
Change in Working Capital					
(Increase) Decr. in Receivables	119.0	230.0	-199.0	-421.5	-486.4
(Increase) Decr. in Inventories	0.0	0.0	0.0	0.0	0.0
(Increase) Decr. in Other Curr. Assets	41.0	-58.0	-124.5	59.8	-102.6
(Decrease) Incr. in Payables	-88.0	-356.0	-13.9	2.8	45.1
(Decrease) Incr. in Other Curr. Liabs.	-12.0	401.0	-682.2	3,413.1	592.9
Other Non-Cash Items	0.0	0.0	0.0	0.0	0.0
Net Cash from Cont. Operations	3,023.0	3,243.0	2,179.1	2,923.6	1,807.1
Net Cash from Discont. Operations	0.0	0.0	0.0	0.0	0.0
Net Cash from Operating Activities	**3,023.0**	**3,243.0**	**2,179.1**	**2,923.6**	**1,807.1**
Cash Flow from Investing Activities					
Cash Flow Provided by:					
Sale of Property, Plant, Equipment	0.0	0.0	0.0	0.0	0.0
Sale of Short Term Investments	5,942.0	4,384.0	725.2	8,517.7	1,080.9
Cash Used by:					
Purchase of Property, Plant, Equipmt.	-291.0	-278.0	-313.3	-263.4	-346.6
Purchase of Short Term Investments	-4,713.0	-6,087.0	-1,583.8	-886.6	-1,250.5
Other Investing Changes Net	-43.0	-157.0	-82.8	-474.6	-286.1
Net Cash from Investing Activities	**895.0**	**-2,138.0**	**-1,254.7**	**6,893.1**	**-802.2**
Cash Flow from Financing Activities					
Cash Flow Provided by:					
Issuance of Debt	9.0	0.0	0.0	0.0	0.8
Issuance of Capital Stock	356.0	332.0	535.9	1,128.3	602.2
Cash Used for:					
Repayment of Debt	0.0	-5.0	-0.1	-4.8	-0.8
Repurchase of Capital Stock	-2,653.0	-2,792.0	-4,340.8	-5,306.8	-1,087.0
Payment of Cash Dividends	0.0	0.0	0.0	0.0	0.0
Other Financing Charges, Net	-166.0	0.0	0.0	0.0	0.0
Net Cash from Financing Activities	**-2,454.0**	**-2,465.0**	**-3,805.0**	**-4,183.2**	**-484.7**
Effect of Exchange Rate Changes	178.0	6.0	-99.4	10.1	-8.1
Net Change in Cash & Cash Equivalents	1,642.0	-1,354.0	-2,980.0	5,643.5	512.0
Cash at Beginning of Period	3,095.0	4,449.0	7,429.2	1,785.7	1,273.7
Free Cash Flow	2,732.0	2,965.0	1,865.8	2,660.2	1,460.5

Statement 3

Look at the Sales figures for Oracle in Statement 1.

Since 2000 was the start of the three-year Bear market, we'll just consider the past three years. Sales from 2001 to 2003 have been declining, however after declining again in 2003, Net Income rose in that year.

The obvious question to ask, then, is how can Net Income improve when Sales are falling?

Looking a little closer we can see that Depreciation and Amortization was much higher in 2002 than in either 2001 or 2003. This caused Net Income to be lower in 2002 although actual sales were higher. This is a good example of why you shouldn't use sales alone as a proxy for how well a company is doing.

Sales can have all sorts of accounting entries applied to them that affect income. In this case the increased write-off of Depreciation isn't a cause for too much concern, but remember, if Sales and Net Income are moving differently or at significantly different rates, you need to determine exactly why this is the case before moving on.

Let's now turn our attention to some of Oracle's key ratios for the last three years' data. Table 2 has the details.

Ratio	2003	2002	2001
Gross Profit Margin	78.7%	78.9%	77.4%
Operating Profit Margin	36.3%	36.9%	34.8%
Net Profit Margin	24.3%	23%	23.6%
Current Ratio	2.22	2.20	2.29
Cash Flow Liquidity Ratio	1.87	1.60	1.69
Debt Ratio	43%	43%	43%
LT Debt to Total Capitalization	3%	5%	5%
Debt to Equity Ratio	0.75	0.77	0.76
Times Interest Earned Ratio	215	178.6	157.4
Cash Flow Margin	0.32	0.34	0.20
ROI	0.21	0.21	0.23
ROE	0.37	0.36	0.41
Cash Return on Assets Ratio	0.27	0.30	0.20

Table 2

Gross Profit Margin, Operating Profit Margin and Net Profit Margin show how well Oracle has translated sales into profits at various stages.

Gross Profit Margin is about the same as its industry competitors, so Oracle is at least keeping up to the industry.

Operating Profit Margin is about 36.3% compared to the industry average of 24%, so Oracle is doing well in that respect.

On the Net Profit Margin front, Oracle's latest figure is 24.3% compared to an industry average of 14.6%. So Oracle is outpacing the industry where it counts (at least from an earnings perspective).

In Oracle's case the profit margins have been either increasing or staying about the same. This is a good sign. If the profit margins had been significantly decreasing, that should raise a flag indicating you need to perform further research to determine the reason.

Oracle's Current Ratio has stayed above 2 times for the past 3 years, so it should have no trouble meeting its short-term debt requirements using only its most liquid assets.

The Cash Flow Liquidity ratio paints a similar picture. When considering Cash Flow from Operating Activities, the ratio is consistent with the Current Ratio and tells us that Oracle has a fairly healthy cash flow it can use to cover its short-term debt.

The Debt ratio gives us the proportion of Oracle's assets that are financed with debt. At a steady 43%, this is reasonable when compared to its industry competitors.

The Long-term Debt to Total Capitalization ratio tells us how Oracle is using long-term debt for its permanent financing. At 3% this shouldn't cause any concerns. Add the fact it has declined from the previous years and we can see that not only is Oracle's relative long-term debt low, but it's getting lower.

The Debt to Equity ratio measures how much money is supplied by creditors, through debt, and by owners, through equity. The higher this ratio, the riskier the company because it is using relatively more debt to finance its operations (and has less of an equity cushion). Oracle's figure (about 0.75 times) is acceptable. You should start to look behind the scenes if the ratio exceeds 1.0 unless management is using its debt well.

The Times Interest Earned value of 215 shows Oracle can more than cover its interest payments from Operating Profit. What's more, this value has been significantly increasing over the past three years, which shows Oracle really doesn't have any debt servicing issues and the situation continues to improve from an already excellent position.

Cash Flow Margin measures the relationship between sales and cash thrown off by operations. Oracle's Cash Flow Margin has increased significantly from 2001 and decreased slightly from 2002. At 32% it is translating sales into cash at a very respectable rate.

Return on Investment (ROI) and Return on Equity (ROE) measure how well the company is managing its investment in assets and generating returns for its owners. ROI shows the profit relative to investment in total assets. With a ROI of 21% compared to an industry value of 7.5% and a ROE of 37% compared to an industry value of 12.1%, Oracle is doing very well. Note however that ROE decreased from its 2001 value – which currently isn't a problem but is worth keeping an eye on.

The final ratio in Table 2, Cash Return on Assets, tells us how much cash Oracle has generated compared to its total assets. Since cash is what's required to pay debt, continue operations and invest in the future, ratios based on actual cash in the bank are useful. At 27%, Oracle is generating a reasonable amount of cash so there are no concerns in this area.

On June 2nd, 2003, Oracle's closing price was 12.80 per share which gave it an Earnings / Price ratio of 3.4% on a fully diluted basis. Since this is well below twice the AAA bond yield that Graham liked to see, you get an inkling that Oracle is not a value stock. In fact, like most technology companies, it's a growth stock whose price factors in relatively large expected future growth.

I'll end Oracle's analysis by comparing Net Income with Cash Flow from Operating Activities over the past three years (see Table 3).

(in millions)	2003	2002	2001
Cash Flow from Operating Activities	3023	3243	2179.1
Net Income	2307	2224	2561.1
Difference	716	1019	(382)

Table 3

Note that Cash Flow from Operating Activities was positive in all three years – a good sign. It was lower than Net Income in 2001, significantly higher in 2002 and somewhat higher in 2003. This tells us that although Oracle's Cash Flow is good, it did not track Income very well. From 2002 to 2003, Cash Flow went down but Income went up. This means that non-cash entries were responsible for the rise in income. As we've seen, this should raise a flag indicating you need to do additional research. In Oracle's case, as it turns out, there was no problem, but you should keep this in mind when analyzing companies.

After completing Oracle's analysis, what conclusions can we draw?

To me it looks like Oracle is a reasonable investment candidate if you like growth stocks, but not so good if your interest lies in value stocks. Then there's what the analysis doesn't tell you: whether Oracle's future prospects in the industry are good.

For example, Oracle has a couple of heavyweight opponents, IBM and Microsoft, that are bent on cutting into its market share for databases. Both companies are well funded, have excellent technical, marketing and management skills and, Microsoft in particular, know how to capture market share.

To a lesser degree, Oracle might face competition from the open source movement. MYSQL is an open source database that currently isn't anywhere near the level of Oracle's offering, however that could change down the road. Just as Linux and Google are starting to give Microsoft fits, MYSQL could be a potential thorn in Oracle's side.

Furthermore, Oracle is making overtures toward the Enterprise Application space where it will compete with the likes of SAP and others. How this strategy eventually turns out is anybody's guess.

Recall the automobile and horse carriage example I mentioned above? These are the types of things you need to consider in addition to analyzing the financial statements and before investing your money.

Remember, you'll have to live with the results, so be sure you've thought of as many potential problems as possible.

At this point you should have an excellent idea on how to analyze stocks in order to find good buys. In essence, this is what Graham did and what Warren Buffett also did in his early years. Of course there are some serious downsides to simply finding cheap stocks, even fundamentally solid ones, and buying them. First, the market could take a very long time to realize these stocks are undervalued. At the end of the day, it doesn't matter whether you own excellent value if nobody is willing to pay you for that value. This is called the *realization-of-value-problem* and is a very real concern, for anyone who invests money in the stock market, because the longer it takes the market to realize the true value of a company, the lower the compounded annual returns will be.

To see why, let's look at an example where a stock that has an intrinsic value of $10 a share is selling at a discounted $5 per share. If the market realizes the stock's true value in a year, the annualized return will be 100%. If it takes two years, the return will be 41.42%. Three years? 25.99%. Five years will return 14.87% and ten years will give a 7.18% return.

As you can see, the differences in annualized returns are significant, and we really don't know when the market will fully value the shares.

Another problem is a company might look attractive at a particular point in time, but a host of intangibles, such as management integrity or government regulation, that weren't reflected in the numbers could cause an excellent business to decline in the future.

To guard against this occurrence, Graham would widely diversify, sometimes holding hundreds of stocks in his portfolio. He expected some would not perform well, but believed the ones that did perform would more than offset the ones that didn't. And he was usually right, as his results often showed.

However Buffett soon tired of this way of thinking and started searching for a more efficient way to invest. He famously said that, "wide diversification is only required when investors do not understand what they are doing." This was not a slight at his mentor Graham, who would have agreed with Buffett, because Graham himself had to admit he did not understand all of the companies he held. There were just too many of them.

Buffett eventually found what he was looking for in the works of John Maynard Keynes, Lawrence Bloomberg and Philip Fisher. When he combined their philosophies with Graham's, he arrived at an investment strategy that has served him well over the past five decades.

Buffett used Keynes' concept of the concentrated portfolio to focus his investment analysis on areas he knew very well, and no others. During the Internet technology boom of the late 90s, Buffett refused to participate and was ridiculed by many for missing out on huge profits. However Buffett had the last laugh when the crash inevitably came. To this day Buffett does not invest in technology firms because he says he doesn't understand their business models.

Bloomberg contributed the idea of the consumer monopoly (or economic moat as we discussed earlier). This is a business that has an extraordinarily high barrier to entry. It could be because of lucrative patents (think pharmaceutical companies), brand (for example, Coca-Cola) or a real monopoly (such as Microsoft Windows). Bloomberg determined such companies should be able to grow their earnings faster, which would lead to higher returns on equity and, eventually, higher share prices. By filtering on this criterion, Buffett was able to eliminate a large number of companies that had higher risks of failing. This one idea allowed Buffett to remove the need to diversify as widely as Graham had because he was relatively certain the companies he chose had a far greater chance of success. Coupled with Keynes' notion of intimately understanding a company's business model, Buffett was at last able to do away with Graham's need to diversify over hundreds of stocks.

Fisher's contribution was the idea of investing only in top-notch businesses and never selling them. This contrasted starkly with Graham's strategy of buying undervalued businesses and then selling them when they reached fair value.

Putting it all together, Buffett now had the seed of his investing strategy. Look for fundamentally solid stocks that represent good value with a built-in margin of safety, invest only in top companies that have a high barrier to entry, only invest in what you know, concentrate your holdings and hold your investments for a very long time.

Of course Buffett added his own ideas to the mix. The book, "Buffettology," by Mary Buffett and David Clark, explains how Buffett views stocks and their earnings.

"In order to understand Warren's view of investing from a business perspective, you must understand that he has a very unorthodox view of a corporation's earnings:

- He considers them his, in proportion to his ownership in the company. So if a company earns $5 a share and Warren owns one hundred shares of the company, he is of the opinion that he has just earned $500.

- Warren also believes that the company has the choice of either paying the $500 out to him via a dividend or retaining those earnings and reinvesting them for him, thus increasing the underlying value of the company. Warren believes that the stock market will, over a period of time, acknowledge this increase in the company's underlying value and cause the stock's price to increase.

This differs from the view most Wall Street professionals hold; they don't consider earnings theirs until the earnings are paid out via dividends."

Because of his view, Buffett can calculate his return by determining what a company will earn in the future. He calculates his initial return by dividing the annual net per share earnings by the share price. So if a company has earned $1 a share and is selling at $10 per share, his initial annual return would be 10%.

But it gets better. Since Buffett is only interested in top-flight companies, he is fairly certain the company's earnings will grow over time. Therefore his returns should increase as time goes by. So if the company earns $1.20 per share next year, Buffett would consider his return to be 12% for that year. And this growth could continue for many years.

But that's not all. It still gets better. By keeping the earnings inside the company (remember that net earnings are after-tax earnings), Buffett's investment compounds year after year tax-free (or at least tax-deferred). If the company had paid out a dividend, that dividend would be taxed in the hands of the investor and thus lose some of its compounding potential.

There are some preconditions however. It should be obvious that for this line of thinking to work, a company needs to have stable and predictable earnings and a long history of growing its per share earnings. This alone removes a sizable number of companies from consideration.

What it all boils down to is companies that have a consistently high return on equity (ROE), and meet the other criteria mentioned above, have the best chance of increasing their share price over the long term. Since the average U.S. company's ROE is about 12%, Buffett looks for an ROE of at least 20%, preferably more.

"Buffettology" contains a list of nine questions to help you determine if an investment is an excellent one or not – I've reprinted them below (I highly recommend the book if you're at all interested in how Buffett invests).

1. Does the business have an identifiable consumer monopoly?
2. Are the earnings of the company strong and showing an upward trend?
3. Is the company conservatively financed (i.e. it has little or no long-term debt and enough cash flow to pay short-term liabilities)?
4. Does the business consistently earn a high rate of return on shareholders' equity?
5. Does the business get to retain its earnings?
6. How much does the business have to spend maintaining current operations?
7. Is the company free to reinvest retained earnings in new business opportunities, expansion of operations, or share repurchases? How good a job does the management do at this?
8. Is the company free to adjust prices to inflation?
9. Will the value added by retained earnings increase the market value of the company?

Assuming you've found a good investment, you then have to take the appropriate action. If your analysis tells you the stock is fundamentally solid and a good buy at the current price (we'll discuss how to determine this in the next chapter), then buy it. Don't let other people, the media or fear mongers dissuade you. If you've done your research and are fully convinced the company is a good one, buy it irrespective of what anyone else is doing. A similar approach should be followed on the sell side. If your research shows the stock should be sold, sell it.

After that you can sit back and enjoy life. Your investments will have a built in margin of safety because you'll have selected only the safest companies representing the best values and purchased them at substantial discounts. And you'll have rid yourself of the risky and overpriced ones.

The margin of safety, popularized by Benjamin Graham, represents the difference between a company's current market value and its intrinsic value when the current value is below the intrinsic value.

For the most part it is far better to buy a company for less than its intrinsic value and wait for the price to catch up, rather than purchasing a company for more than it's worth and waiting for its value to catch up.

Follow these principles and your investments should generally be moving ahead faster than if you had continually bought and sold stocks in a haphazard manner. Plus you'll spend less time and energy on your portfolio because you'll have harnessed the power of pragmatic investing and compounding over time.

Of course you might still need to make minor course corrections along the way in order to wring out the best possible returns or, perhaps, to take advantage of other investors' errors (such as when they drive up prices on a stock you own to unrealistic levels).

So while most investors will continually miss good values, follow poor investment strategies and ignore fundamentals, recall that you are not "most" investors. No, you belong to an elite group of people that know how to determine a company's fundamental strength and calculate a realistic valuation. You are prepared and know how to take the correct action and reap the rewards of a financially sound future. In short, you're a **Pragmatic Investor.**

Not at all bad for spending a day at the beach. Of course even great companies can be overpriced, so before you jump in and purchase shares in that excellent company you just found, you need to ensure you are buying at a price that will give you a sufficient Margin of Safety.

So pick up your beach towel and come in from the sun while we discuss exactly how to do that in the next chapter.

ACTION PLAN

Go through your portfolio and check the fundamentals of EACH stock you own. If they don't measure up, get rid of them. Find replacements that are good values and have excellent fundamental foundations.

Chapter Eleven

Stock Valuation

"Price is what you pay. Value is what you get."

Benjamin Graham

I n the previous chapter we discussed how to determine whether a company was worth purchasing by asking a series of important questions, looking at its fundamentals and determining its moat strength.

So assuming you're happy with the company so far, you've done your research, like the answers to the questions you asked and like the fundamentals, what's next?

Valuation. That's what.

Just because a company is fundamentally solid, doesn't mean you should jump in and purchase it without first asking yourself two very important semi-related questions:

1) Is it too expensive at its current price?
2) What price should I pay for it?

Now there are a number of methods available for determining a company's intrinsic value, and I'll discuss two of the more common methods as we make our way through this chapter, but the one I use the most is based on Earnings per Share (EPS).

Note there are a number of pitfalls in using this approach, the chief one being that it relies on estimating the EPS growth out into the future – usually for at least the next 5 years.

Be aware that not all companies have predictable EPS growth. In fact, a large majority do not. However there is good news. The fundamentally solid companies value investors should be looking at generally have stable and predictable businesses and thus stable and predictable earnings. And since we're usually not interested in fundamentally weak businesses, the EPS method of determining a company's intrinsic value generally works well.

But your mileage may vary and depends on the types of stocks that catch your attention.

Okay, so with that prologue out of the way, let's dive in and find some intrinsic value.

As an example, I'll use Moody's Corporation (MCO) since Warren Buffett holds a big chunk of it, through his various companies, and, in the past, has said it is a great company. The thing is, he might be having second thoughts in today's economic climate.

During July of 2009, Buffett sold about 16% of his stake. Nonetheless, he still holds about 17% of the company even after his recent divestiture. So Moody's it is.

Before we can begin, we'll need some data. We'll need the company's **current Earnings Per Share** (EPS), its **annual Dividend payment** (if any) and the average analysts' estimates of its **Future EPS Growth** to estimate what the stock will be worth in the future. You can find all these data items at Microsoft's Money Central site.

In MCO's case, the numbers as of July 2009 are:

EPS = $1.68, Dividend = $0.40 and 5-year estimated growth rate = 12 %.

Next we'll need to determine how long to hold the stock. Longer periods are better, but the issue here is that the longer you project, the less accurate your EPS growth rate estimates might become. But then again, if you're dealing with a top-flight company, your estimates might end up being even more accurate.

In any event, we'll use 5 years for our calculations. Using these data, we can calculate the future value of EPS for the 5-year time period using the following formula:

$$\text{Future EPS} = P(1 + r)^{\wedge}Y + c[\ ((1 + r)^{\wedge}(Y + 1) - (1 + r))\ /\ r\ ]$$

Where P = the current EPS; r = Est. EPS Growth; c = ½ the dividend rate; Y = Years to Hold.

Note that we use ½ the dividend rate rather than the entire amount, because dividends are not guaranteed and they can be reduced or eliminated at any time. So by using half the current dividend, we start building a very conservative estimate of the Future EPS value.

Therefore,

MCO's Future EPS = 1.68 (1.12) ^5 + 0.20[((1.12)^ 6 - (1.12)) / 0.12]
= 4.38

So Moody's Future EPS is $4.38.

Once we have the future EPS value, we can now estimate the future price for the stock by using the **Lowest Average P/E ratio** over the past 5 years (17.80 for MCO). Again, we want to build a conservative estimate and therefore we err on the side of caution whenever possible.

We can calculate the estimated future price using the following formula:

Estimated Future Price = Future EPS * Lowest Average P/E for past 5 Years

So,

MCO's estimated future price = 4.38 x 17.80 = $77.96

Once the Future Price has been estimated, the next step is to discount that price back to the present day. The formula to do this is:

Price = FP / (1 + r)^Y

Where FP = the Future Price; r = Discount Rate; Y = Years to Hold.

To determine the correct Discount Rate, we need to decide on the Margin of Safety and expected Worst Case Return we require.

The formula to calculate the Discount Rate is:

Discount Rate = Worst Case Return / (1 – Margin of Safety)

Plugging in all the numbers gives us the maximum price we should be willing to pay today in order to have the required Margin of Safety and worst case return.

If the stock's current price is less than or equal to the maximum purchase price we calculated, then we should be happy to purchase the stock. Otherwise we should pass, as the stock is currently too expensive.

Note the higher the Margin of Safety and the Worst Case Return we decide upon, the fewer stocks will meet these criteria. Lower settings will return more stocks.

You can use any Margin of Safety and Worst Case Return values, but the recommend values are 50% and 12% respectively.

You can interpret this to mean that if the stock's return drops 50% from what you expect, your return will be 12% annually.

If the stock returns what you expect, you'll see a 24% return.

The reason we use a worst-case return of 12% is because this is the average annual return of the S&P 500 over long periods of time.

If you're going to spend the time and effort investing in individual stocks, you should expect to do MUCH better than the S&P 500 (the goal should be to at least double the S&P 500's return). If you can't do that, then you're better off investing in a low-cost S&P 500 index fund.

Plugging in the data based on our 50% Margin of Safety and 12% worst-case return, our discount rate becomes:

$$0.12 \ / \ (1 - 0.5) = 0.24$$

So our maximum buy price is:

$$77.96 \ / \ (1.24) \ {}^\wedge 5 = \$26.59$$

At the time of writing MCO is trading at $23.86. So it looks like the company is a buy (assuming its fundamentals are strong).

What you might have noticed is there are an awful lot of calculations required in order to find the intrinsic value of ONE STOCK! And you're right. It's also error prone. But that's how it was done for decades before computers came onto the scene.

Nowadays you can simply use a **Compound Interest** calculator to determine the Future EPS value and use a **Present Value** calculator to determine the maximum purchase price. Or better yet, use a spreadsheet. Or even better, use the **Pragmatic Investor** software that does it all for you.

But I digress.

Back to the topic of valuation, let me say there usually won't be a very large number of high quality stocks trading at a discount with a sufficient Margin of Safety at any particular time.

However you can find a handful if you're disciplined and patient. Using the Value Investing approach, you can actually pick up these bargains when others are jumping out of them for any number of short-term reasons.

And when you do, you position yourself to profit handsomely.

Nevertheless, the only way you can achieve these types of returns (and safety margins) is to be patient and pay less than what most people pay. In other words, the price you pay for a stock will determine the return you can expect on your investment.

The less you pay, the greater your return. The more you pay, the lower your return.

And that is what Benjamin Graham meant when he talked about the Margin of Safety.

Of course the valuation technique I've just described is not the only method, and Warren Buffett likes to use another method based on the Return on Equity (ROE).

To see Buffett's method in action, let's look at another example – we'll use Marvel Entertainment (MVL) this time. It's close to rating Very Good on the **fundamentals scale** we discussed in the last chapter – but it's not quite there, it has a strong **moat rating** of 5, an **average ROE** over the past 5 years of 40.64% and it retains all of its earnings – that is, it pays no dividends. Further MVL has a **per share equity value** of $5.08 and its lowest **average P/E ratio** over the past 5 years is 11.60.

Given these data, we can now estimate what the company should be worth 5 years from now. First, we calculate the projected per share equity value 5 years hence. The present value is $5.08, the 5-year average ROE is 40.64% and the number of years is 5.

Plugging these values into a Compound Interest calculator spits out a future value of $27.95. In 5 years the company is projected to have a per share equity value of $27.95.

To estimate the per share earnings 5 years in the future, we simply multiply this $27.95 value by the 40.64% ROE to get a projected per share earnings value of $11.36.

To estimate the share price in 5 years, multiply $11.36 by 11.60 (MVL's lowest 5-year average P/E) to get $131.78.

Now we can discount that future price back to the present using exactly the same method we used in the Moody's example above. Assuming our recommended discount rate of 24%, we can calculate our maximum buy price to be:

$$\$131.78 \,/\, (1.24)\; {}^{\wedge}5 = \$44.95$$

Since MVL is currently trading at $39.01, it looks like a buy – at least from a valuation perspective but you still have to do your due diligence and ensure you're happy with the results.

(As a side note, a few months after I had written this section on MVL's valuation, Disney, ticker DIS, purchased MVL, in 2009, for more than $50 per share – combined cash and DIS shares.)

Keep in mind both of the valuation methods we've just seen rely on forecasts going out into the future. If you're looking at a company that has a spotty or volatile earnings or ROE history, these methods can end up being very inaccurate.

However, as I mentioned earlier, the companies you should be looking at (those with superior fundamentals and strong moats) should all have consistent earnings and ROE. So these valuation strategies should work well with them (but as usual, don't blindly follow formulas without injecting your own common sense).

For a stronger strategy, you can use both valuation methods and either average the results to find a maximum buy price or, for the more conservative investor, use the lower of the two as your maximum.

The point is to make your purchasing decision based on facts, logic and the numbers rather than on emotions, hype and the need to see action. If you want to do well in the stock market, you need to take a page out of Buffett's book and follow his lead.

Now if you've read this far, you have the tools and knowledge necessary to invest better than 99.99% of all investors in the world. I know it can be hard to believe, but the vast majority of investors actually put their money on the line knowing next to nothing or, perhaps worse, trusting "professional" money managers. You no longer need to be part of that group. In fact if you read no further you'll most likely do quite well just by following what we've discussed so far.

However we're not quite finished. In the next chapter we'll look at a strategy designed to wring out even more value by taking advantage of short-term volatility while still adhering to the long-term value investing tenets. After that, we'll look at managing risk at the portfolio level through concentrated diversification and asset allocation. Once you understand these last two concepts and are able to use the tools necessary to implement them, you'll be among the very elite of stock market investors.

ACTION PLAN

Before you purchase any new stock, calculate the maximum purchase price as outlined in this chapter. If the current price is greater than the calculated maximum buy price, don't buy it.

Either wait for the price to fall or move onto another stock. Ensure you do this before making any new buying decisions.

Chapter Twelve
Value Trading Algorithm

"In the short term the market is a popularity contest;
in the long term it is a weighing machine."

Warren Buffett

You've no doubt heard about various rebalancing strategies and how rebalancing is the key to buying low and selling high. Of course when people speak of rebalancing, they're usually talking about the long-term.

But there's a short-term version you can use to take advantage of short-term market volatility. In fact historical testing has shown, that with a group of volatile stocks, the increase in returns can be quite substantial.

I've called this short-term rebalancing technique the **Value Trading Algorithm** to distinguish it from its long-term sibling.

So how does it work?

First, it is not meant to reduce risk at all. It doesn't expect to increase risk, but neither does it expect to decrease it. Rather it focuses solely on increasing returns (that's why it should always be used with the regular long-term diversification, allocation and rebalancing techniques that will be covered in the next chapter). I purposely chose to put the term *Value* in its name to remind users the stocks used with this technique <u>must</u> be solid and fundamentally sound. In addition they <u>should</u> be undervalued so that the built-in margin of safety helps to reduce the risk (since the strategy itself doesn't).

Second, it is a short-term strategy that can significantly increase the number of trades you make. However the increase in trades is generally accompanied by an increase in returns (thus the term *Trading* in its name). But keep in mind that by trading more frequently you open yourself to not only increased trading fees, but also potential increased taxes and short-term capital gains. For these reasons it might be better to use this strategy in a tax-free (such as the Canadian TFSA) or tax-deferred account.

It's also important to understand this technique **must** be used as part of the overall strategy I've been explaining in this book. Although it might be tempting to use it alone, this is not recommended.

With these warnings out of the way, let's see how the Value Trading Algorithm works. We'll start by creating a group of four or more highly correlated stocks with similar expected returns (again, these stocks must be selected for their strong fundamentals and should also be undervalued). A good way to start is by grouping stocks from the same industry together. I'll call this the micro-level.

Once we have this group, we need to realize two important things: (i) over the long-term, stock prices for this group will tend to move together (that's the definition of *highly correlated*), (ii) over the short-term, stock prices in this group will probably diverge, sometimes to a great degree (even highly correlated stocks don't follow each other exactly over short periods of time).

To start, we'll invest all of our funds in one stock in the group. As prices diverge, we monitor all the stocks in the group to see if any of the ones that we don't own have underperformed the one we do own by more than some set percentage.

When that happens we sell our current stock and purchase the underperforming one. Since we know over the long-term all stocks in the group behave similarly, it follows that either the underperformer (the one we just purchased) will rise or the over-performer (the one we just sold) will drop, usually in a relatively short period of time. Either way, we're better off holding the underperforming stock. We then reset our monitoring and repeat the process.

You'll note there are a couple of differences between this short-term rebalancing micro-level technique and the regular, long-term rebalancing strategy we'll discuss in the next chapter.

First, we rebalance in an extreme way – that is, our allocation is 100% in one stock at any given time. Contrast this to a long-term rebalancing strategy where we rebalance back to a specific portfolio allocation with a set percentage in each one of many stocks.

Second, all stocks in the group are highly correlated and as a direct result we don't reduce risk.

What does happen is we can dramatically boost returns by capturing the short-term volatility inherent in the group of stocks. This short-term volatility would otherwise be wasted, so we're generally no worse off risk-wise, but far better off return-wise.

Of course we don't simply use one group of stocks. Rather we create 8 to 20 groups (each with 4 or more highly correlated stocks) where the correlations *between* each group are as low as possible while the correlations *within* each group are as high as possible. If we have, for example, 10 groups each containing 4 stocks, our universe will consist of 40 potential selections. However we will only be invested in 10 stocks (one from each group) at any particular point in time.

Keep in mind all stocks in our universe must have scored well on our fundamental filters tests and be fundamentally solid with strong moats. The reason is because we are always going to be invested in some of them and therefore will end up holding at least some for a long time, but we won't be able to predict which ones we'll hold – so it's imperative they are all excellent stocks.

Conceptually we can treat each group as a single position for the purposes of diversification, allocation and regular rebalancing (I'll call these the macro-levels). The macro-level techniques do not need to know we might be switching between individual stocks in each group (that is, rebalancing at the micro-level), because over the long-term, all individual stocks in the same group should behave similarly – since they are highly correlated.

The net result is, when coupled with macro-level techniques, the Value Trading Algorithm helps to increase returns by ensuring the most efficient use of all types of volatility (both long-term and short-term) and is an important part of any Pragmatic Investor's investment strategy.

The main concept to take away from all of this is that every one of our techniques (whether at the micro- or macro-level) *react* to what the market does rather than trying to predict it.

But let's get back to the Value Trading Algorithm and see how it performed with a group of Canadian banking stocks. In 2009, Canadian banks were rated as the best banks in the world. Suffice it to say, these are some of the finest blue-chip and fundamentally solid stocks in Canada (and the world). They scored extremely well on the fundamentals filters tests and all have strong moats. They were also severely undervalued in the latter part of 2008 and first quarter of 2009 (mainly because of a knee-jerk reaction many investors had to anything having to do with banks during that time).

In addition, as a group, they're highly correlated. The five major Canadian banks are Royal Bank (RY), TD Canada Trust (TD), Bank of Montreal (BMO), Canadian Imperial Bank of Commerce (CM) and Bank of Nova Scotia (BNS).

So how did they do when used with the Value Trading Algorithm (VTA) compared to a simple Buy and Hold (B&H) strategy? Table 4 contains the results for periods covering 13 years, 10 years, 7 years, 5 years, 3 years and 1 year.

Period	VTA Annual Return (%)	B&H Annual Return (%)
8/14/1996 to 8/14/2009	28.47	14.51
8/14/1999 to 8/14/2009	24.55	11.64
8/14/2002 to 8/14/2009	19.41	11.45
8/14/2004 to 8/14/2009	20.81	8.86
8/14/2006 to 8/14/2009	18.46	2.66
8/14/2008 to 8/14/2009	70.54	9.93

Table 4

As you can see, the Value Trading Algorithm significantly outperformed the Buy and Hold strategy in every single period. Note also the recent one-year period, starting in August 2008, included the worst economic crisis since the Great Depression – and as a result, the stock market was extremely volatile. The Value Trading Algorithm was able to capture that extreme volatility and returned an astounding 70.54% compared to 9.93% for Buy and Hold.

In fact, $10,000 invested on August 14th, 1996 would have grown to $259,670.38 by August 14, 2009 using the Value Trading Algorithm compared to just $58,205.55 with the Buy and Hold strategy. That's more than 4 times the Buy and Hold value and an **extra** $201,464.83 that would have been lost without VTA. It should be clear that not using short-term volatility to your advantage can be very costly indeed.

And the nice thing is that at no time was the VTA portfolio invested in anything other than high-quality blue-chip companies. Of course to properly take advantage of this strategy, we would build at least 7 more groups and let VTA manage each group independently.

And if you're wondering why we just don't work with one group of stocks, it's for the same reason we would not want to hold just one stock in a regular non-Value-Trading-Algorithm managed portfolio: RISK.

Even well selected, fundamentally solid stocks can bite you. And that's why all smart investors diversify, optimize and rebalance their portfolios. The question is how to do these things correctly in order to minimize risk. And that's exactly what we'll look at in the next chapter.

ACTION PLAN

Try to find 4 or 5 highly correlated, fundamentally solid stocks and group them together. Repeat until you have at least 8 groups where every group has a low correlation with every other group.

Once you've done that, manage each group independently, with the Value Trading Algorithm, so you have the highest probability of increasing your returns by taking advantage of the market's inherent short-term volatility.

Chapter Thirteen

Risk

"Risk comes from not knowing what you are doing."

Warren Buffett

O nce your stock has passed the fundamental analysis tests, you can be reasonably confident you have a good long-term investment. However sometimes even good stocks turn bad.

To combat this possibility, **Pragmatic Investors** have long used the age-old principle of not putting all their eggs into one basket. In a word, they diversify.

But is diversification really that important?

Absolutely! Diversification is the primary tool you can use to spread your risk between countries, currencies and markets. It allows you to take advantage of opportunities when they unexpectedly appear and protects you from unseen crises situations. In short, diversification reduces risk and, when properly applied, can increase returns.

But isn't that what mutual funds are supposed to do? Theoretically, yes. In reality, No.

There's ample research that shows two things very clearly.

First, most active money managers don't beat the market over ten years or more. How much is "most?" Try over 80%.

The problem is that after deducting all of their trading and marketing expenses, management fees and other charges (such as loads), they have to earn substantially more than the market **just to break even**.

Coupled with the fact most funds have hundreds of millions of dollars to invest and caps on how much they can invest in any one stock, it's easy to see why so many have trouble just consistently keeping up with the market indexes, let alone beating them.

And as we've seen, actively managed mutual fund managers tend to focus on the short-term thereby giving up huge long-term profits.

Second, those that end up beating the market can't be identified in advance.

Therefore, in order to stack the deck in your favor, to position your portfolio so it's most probable you do well, you can't depend on actively managed mutual funds. Rather you need to properly diversify and implement an asset allocation strategy that works.

But how do you diversify properly? What investments should you include? How many different investments should you have in your portfolio? What percentage should each contribute to your portfolio's overall make up?

These are all important questions, but people didn't know the answers for many years.

It took until the 1950s for someone to actually quantify how to distribute your eggs into the different baskets. That someone was **Harry Markowitz**, and for his efforts he would eventually be awarded a Nobel Prize in Economics.

As we shall see, Markowitz's work on Modern Portfolio Theory (MPT) revolutionized how investors started to think about investing. No longer were they concerned with just returns, but now risk entered the picture. And since Markowitz showed how to measure risk, as surely as returns, it was now possible, for the first time, to compare portfolios and determine which ones were riskier.

This in turn has a profound effect on how today's **Pragmatic Investor** views his portfolio. Rather than viewing each investment as an independent unit, discrete and separate from his other investments, individual investments are viewed as part of the whole portfolio. The interactions between investments become important and properly selected investments can provide synergies that can increase returns while at the same time minimizing risk.

In other words, there are good ways to diversify and bad ways. Markowitz showed us how we could distinguish between the two.

Unfortunately the underlying calculations required to implement his theory were onerous and not conducive to solving by hand. Therefore it wasn't until the late 1970s, when computers started to show up everywhere, that MPT took off.

Attesting to its validity is the fact a large number of professional money managers now use MPT to help them with their work.

The important insight of MPT is that the risk of an individual asset is not too important. What is of prime importance is its contribution to the portfolio's risk as a whole. And that's why MPT uses diversification as its primary mechanism.

Before we delve into the intricacies of MPT, however, let's pause a moment to look at investment risk.

I'm a huge hockey fan. I think it's the greatest game on Earth. And the 1980s had one of the greatest teams to ever play the game, the Edmonton Oilers – home of Wayne Gretzky.

That's the same Gretzky who lit up scoreboards across the National Hockey League with his uncanny timing, deft passing and mesmerizing presence.

No other hockey player scored more goals or had more assists than the man they dubbed, "the Great One."

To be sure, the spotlight was on Gretzky. Once scoring an unprecedented 92 goals and adding another 120 assists in just 80 games, he redefined the term, "hockey superstar."

Gretzky led his Edmonton Oilers to 4 NHL championships and had four 200+ point seasons. No other athlete, with the exception of Michael Jordan and perhaps Tiger Woods, dominated his sport like Gretzky.

Meanwhile, with the glare of the spotlight constantly showering Gretzky, a lone goaltender named Grant Fuhr stood patiently in the net, night after night, backstopping Gretzky's team to championship after championship.

However unless you're a hockey fan or grew up in Edmonton, you probably never heard of Grant Fuhr, but without Fuhr, Edmonton would not have won a single championship – even with the Great Gretzky presiding.

So what do Gretzky and Fuhr have to do with investing and risk?

Well, Gretzky was the team's offence. He scored the goals and racked up the points. When the media reported on a game, you always heard about Gretzky's points.

Fuhr, on the other hand, was the team's defense. You rarely heard about Fuhr, but if he wasn't a great goaltender, Edmonton would have lost game after game after game. To be a great team over the long-term, Edmonton needed both Gretzky's offence and Fuhr's defense.

Similarly investments need a balance of both offence and defense. Investors must concentrate as much on risk as they do on returns if they hope to achieve long-term success.

Without factoring risk into the investment equation, long-term results will not only under-perform the averages, but might even end up being zero. Just ask some investors (and I use the term loosely) who concentrated solely on returns during the Internet stock IPO heyday.

Those that managed their risk, however, were able to participate in the upside and save their portfolios from the markets' eventual demise.

Back in the late nineties it seemed that every mutual fund company took out full-page advertisements, in financial newspapers, touting their funds' returns. Annual returns of eighty, ninety and 100% were not uncommon. Missing, unfortunately, were the risk figures.

This is what I call the **Gretzky phenomenon**. A phenomenon where the entire focus is placed on the most visible and exciting part of a system while ignoring other, just as important, pieces.

In the nineties, the media spotlight was squarely shining on returns, much like it did on Gretzky's results, and ignoring the associated risks. Falling prey to the Gretzky phenomenon is a dangerous thing and will, in all probability, set the stage for catastrophic failure.

Today, in hindsight, we can see that focusing solely on returns was a HUGE mistake that ultimately cost investors billions of dollars.

The Edmonton Oilers had it right when they used Fuhr to support Gretzky's accomplishments. And successful investors also had it right when they used risk management tools to support their stellar returns.

So what are these tools? Before we delve into that area let's look at how we measure risk.

There are many ways to measure risk, but one of the most popular is a statistical term called the standard deviation. You can think of it as the uncertainty you have that your expected return will be what you predict. Let's say you believe, based on historical data, IBM will return 9% annually over the next 10 years. You can't be certain of this, but you have a good feeling. The standard deviation measures the probability you're right.

Therefore high standard deviations mean you have a greater chance of being wrong while low standard deviations mean you have a lower chance of being wrong – or a greater chance of being right.

If you invested your money in some kind of government guaranteed instrument, such as a treasury bill, your expected return would be whatever the effective interest rate was when you bought it. Since the government guarantees it, you'll receive exactly that return – assuming the Government doesn't fail, but in that unlikely scenario you'll have much more to worry about than your expected return.

Therefore the standard deviation of your government-backed investment is zero (i.e. there is no uncertainty as to your expected return). If however you invest in a risky penny-stock, the standard deviation would be quite high. You would have very low confidence in your expected future return (i.e. there is a high degree of uncertainty as to your expected return).

Keep in mind that the standard deviation does not measure risk in all situations. Special occurrences, such as Enron's collapse, are risks that are outside the standard deviation's ability to measure.

There might also be other circumstances where the standard deviation might not be valid, but overall it is a fairly good measure of risk because it tells you how "risky" your chosen stock has been in the past and, ceteris paribus, is likely to be in the future.

Now that we know how to measure risk, what exactly are we measuring? Risk comes in two flavors: Market risk (systematic risk) and specific risk (unsystematic risk). If you invest in the stock market then you can't do anything about Market risk, however you can minimize specific risk.

An example of specific risk is if the company in which you invested all of your funds declares bankruptcy and its shares are now worthless. You've just been the victim of specific risk, but you didn't have to be. The simple act of diversifying your portfolio can shield you from specific risk.

Diversifying within a particular industry is good, but diversifying over a number of industries is better. So rather than have all your assets in technology stocks, you could also purchase banking stocks and consumer stocks.

But what exactly do you buy? And how do you split up your portfolio? Do you put equal amounts of money in each stock? In each industry? What do you do?

Fortunately these questions can be easily answered. First you need to decide which stocks to hold in your portfolio. You can choose them based on instinct, but there is a better way.

Ideally you want to hold stocks that behave differently from one another. So when one of your stocks is going down, another is going up. This serves to insulate your portfolio from wild and terrifying swings in value.

To measure this we use another statistical term called correlation. Stocks that are positively correlated have a high probability of moving together. Therefore if stock A and stock B are positively correlated, we can expect stock B's price to increase whenever stock A's price increases. Similarly both should decrease at the same time.

On the other hand, if the stocks are negatively correlated, then when stock A's price increases, we would expect stock B's price to decrease – and vice versa. Stocks that are neither positively nor negatively correlated move randomly with respect to each other.

Once you determine your stocks' correlation matrix, you can select the ones that should be in your portfolio (you want to choose the ones with low positive, or better yet negative, correlations – the **Pragmatic Investor** software's Asset Allocation feature lists correlations for you).

Note that I haven't said anything about fundamental analysis – and that's an important point. These techniques do absolutely nothing to determine if the stocks you hold are good or bad.

You have to perform your own due diligence and fundamental analysis before selecting potential candidates (the **Pragmatic Investor** software's Fundamental Analyzer can give you a good start).

So now that you know which stocks to include, what's next?

You can calculate a stock's standard deviation, over some time period, from its historical data. You can then use this standard deviation to plot a chart of that stock's risk versus its expected return.

If you do this for all the stocks in your portfolio, you'll have a chart showing each stock's risk versus reward (normally we define risk on the x-axis and expected return on the y-axis).

You then have to determine the level of risk you're willing to take in order to achieve an expected return. Normally you'd minimize your risk level for a given return or maximize your return for a given risk level.

For example, let's say I was looking to achieve a 10% annual return in the stock market. Let's also say there were two stocks with expected returns of 10%, stock A, which had a standard deviation of 30%, and stock B, with a standard deviation of 10%. Which would I choose?

If you've been following everything so far, your answer should be stock B. That's because it gives me the same expected return as stock A, but with much less risk (i.e. its standard deviation is much less than stock A's).

That's easy to see with only two separate stocks, but how do you determine the correct choices based on a portfolio that might contain 10 or 20 individual stocks?

There are a number of ways, which we'll see shortly, but the granddaddy of risk management tools is the portfolio optimizer.

The optimizer's job is to take all of the stocks in your portfolio and create a set of **Efficient Portfolios**. These are the portfolios that have the smallest amount of risk for a given return or the greatest return for a given risk level.

This is similar to the example above, with two stocks, except this time we're working with an entire portfolio of multiple stocks and we take the correlations between stocks into account.

Efficient portfolios combine to form the Efficient Frontier. All portfolios that lie on the efficient frontier are called efficient portfolios.

An example is shown in Figure 1.

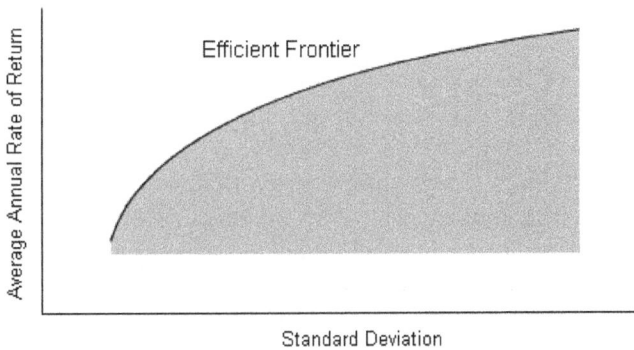

Figure 1

Portfolios below the Efficient Frontier curve (shaded area) are not efficient in that there is a better portfolio available, one that has a higher expected return for the same risk level or a lower risk level for the same expected return.

Portfolios above the Efficient Frontier curve are not attainable with the given stocks. For example you cannot expect to achieve a 100% return with zero risk.

After the portfolio optimizer has finished, you can select a portfolio from the set it returns. Each portfolio will have a different risk versus reward characteristic. So if you're looking to achieve a 10% return, the portfolio you select will have the minimum possible risk required to achieve that return.

Similarly if you're looking to limit your risk to 5%, the portfolio you choose will be the one that maximizes your return at that risk level.

Once you've selected a portfolio, you'll see exactly how much of each stock to put into your portfolio in order to achieve your desired return or risk level. An example might be 10% of your portfolio invested in IBM, 5% invested in Yahoo!, 20% invested in GE, 35% invested in treasury bills and 30% invested in the Bank of Montreal.

MPT, therefore, quantifies risk relative to expected return and provides a mathematical model that shows you the best portfolio (how best to combine the individual investments in your portfolio) to use for a given level of risk or return.

Using these risk-management techniques allow you to diversify your portfolio based on historically confirmed, time-tested methods rather than on emotion and ad hoc strategies.

Let's now delve into the details, the actual methods you can use to allocate assets.

There are a number of strategies that have been, and continue to be, used. They range from completely useless to very good. I'll mention three of the better ones.

The simplest way to diversify is to decide which stocks you'd like to own and divide your investment funds equally between them. Then, periodically, you rebalance. This diversification strategy is better than nothing, but lacks any real ability to use synergies that might be present in your portfolio.

A better method is to use the **Sharpe ratio**. The Sharpe Ratio is a measure of reward to risk. The higher the value, the better the investment (from a reward/risk perspective).

Note a high Sharpe Ratio doesn't necessarily mean the highest return or the lowest risk. Rather it means that's the best you could have done when reward and risk were taken together.

To calculate the Sharpe Ratio you need a stock's Expected Return and Standard Deviation. You also need the best risk-free rate (typically the interest rate of U.S. Treasuries). The Sharpe Ratio calculation is given in Equation 1.

```
S(x) = ( rx  -  Rf ) / StdDev(x)

x is an investment (e.g. IBM).
rx is the average annual rate of return of x.

Rf is the best available rate of return of a "risk-
free" security (i.e. U.S. Treasuries).

StdDev(x) is the standard deviation of rx.
```

Equation 1

Graphically, the Sharpe Ratio looks like this:

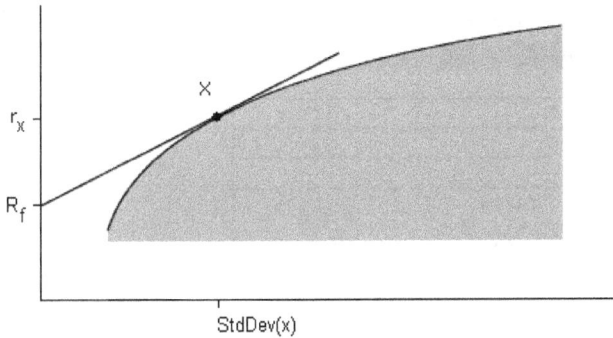

Figure 2

The slope of the straight line is equal to the Sharpe Ratio of security x.

Once you've calculated the Sharpe Ratio for each stock in your portfolio, you can use a simple method to diversify more intelligently than just throwing equal amounts of cash at your stocks.

Here are the steps.

1. Compute the Sharpe Ratio for each stock in your portfolio (as described above).
2. Sum all of the Sharpe Ratio values.
3. Divide each stock's Sharpe Ratio by the sum of the Sharpe Ratios. This gives the percentage allocation for that stock.

For example, let's say you have 3 stocks in your portfolio (A, B and C) each with the Sharpe ratio listed in Table 5 on the next page.

Stock	Sharpe Ratio
A	2.5
B	1.5
C	4.0
Sharpe Ratio Sum	8.0

Table 5

In this case, the sum of the Sharpe Ratios is 8 (i.e. 2.5 + 1.5 + 4.0 = 8).

Divide the Sharpe Ratio for stock A by the sum of 8 to get 2.5/8 = 0.3125 (or about 31%).

Do the same for B and C, and you'll get 0.1875 (approximately 19%) and 0.5 (50%) respectively.

The results indicate that you should invest about 31% of your money in stock A, about 19% in stock B and 50% in stock C.

The advantage of this strategy is that the better reward-to-risk stocks get a larger share of your investment funds (which is a far more logical way to go than the simple equal allocation strategy described above. Note the **Pragmatic Investor** software uses this method to diversify portfolios).

However the strategy doesn't take into account the possible interactions between securities in a portfolio. But these interactions can be significant (for example, adding a risky stock to a less-risky portfolio can actually cause the entire portfolio's risk to *decrease*).

And that's where Markowitz's MPT enters the picture. MPT seeks to provide portfolios, consisting of various weightings of stocks, that maximize return for a given risk or minimize risk for a given return.

Calculating these portfolios require you to have the Mean and Standard Deviation for a stock as well as a Covariance matrix (which is just a table that lists how stocks behave relative to one another). You can also get by with

Correlation Coefficients (which you can then use to calculate the Covariances).

The first step in using MPT is to predict each investment's expected return and standard deviation over the long-term (we can generally come up with a good prediction if we're dealing with long periods of time).

Next you'll need the correlation data that indicates how an individual stock moves with respect to the other stocks in your portfolio. There will be one number for each pair of stocks.

All of this information can be obtained from an investment's historical data. Once we have these data, we can begin our MPT calculations. Our goal is to diversify our investments, in very specific portions, in order to come up with a portfolio that provides a given return at the lowest risk level or the best return for a given level of risk.

MPT assumes investors will always want the highest return at the lowest risk. In essence it asks, "why would an investor choose an asset that returns 4% a year with a 50% chance of losing some money over an investment that returns the same 4% a year with a 0.001% chance of losing some money?"

The answer, of course, is that a rational investor would not do this. Instead he would choose the investment that returns 4% with the 0.001% risk level. Of course some investors might choose an investment that returns 5% with a 50% risk of losing money over the 4% return, 0.001% risk level investment.

And that's okay with MPT. It doesn't make assumptions in those cases. If investors are willing to accept greater risk, then they must be compensated with greater returns (no matter how much smaller or how much greater).

MPT takes advantage of the fact that while the expected return of a portfolio is simply the weighted average expected return of the individual stocks that make up that portfolio, the portfolio's standard deviation can be less than the average standard deviation of the individual stocks – if you choose stocks that aren't highly correlated.

Therefore many savvy investors diversify by investing in foreign markets as well as different industries and investment classes. The key point is to choose investments that aren't highly correlated. This happens to be the case with domestic securities and foreign ones.

Interestingly enough, rather than making your own portfolio selection, you can use the Sharpe Ratio to automatically select the best portfolio.

This frees you from worrying about what risk you're willing to assume or what minimum return you'd like.

Once MPT has returned the set of efficient portfolios, you calculate the Sharpe Ratio for each one and choose the one with the highest Sharpe Ratio. It's easy and it's automatic. Your computer can even do it for you.

However before you get too excited, there is a very real problem when using MPT in the real world.

The problem stems from Markowitz's assumptions you are able to accurately estimate standard deviations, covariances and means.

This is a flawed assumption.

If your estimates happen to be off by just little (especially for the means), the resulting asset allocation can be significantly different. It's hard enough to obtain a reasonable mean and standard deviation, but adding covariance values (you need one between each pair of stocks) just increases the odds that you won't get something quite right.

The problem of a small change in input creating a large change in output is known more commonly as the **Butterfly Effect**. MPT suffers from the Butterfly Effect in a serious way.

It can tell you exactly how you should have diversified to obtain the best results, however it can fail spectacularly when trying to predict how to diversify for the future.

Having said that, however, MPT can work reasonably well if you use it with index funds over long periods of time.

If you're investing in individual stocks, you should forget about MPT and allocate using the Sharpe ratio method I described earlier.

There's also another problem with the theories I've just described. Markowitz used proven statistical methods in his theories. And they would work very well if the stock market followed a normal distribution.

However it doesn't. Most of the time it looks like it does, and that unfortunately lulls many investors into a false sense of security. Let's explore why this is so.

First, you need to understand that markets are dynamic and unpredictable. Most of the time they can seem to be well behaved and our minds can trick us into believing that. However the truth is far different. If rare events happen with asymmetric payoffs, this can wipe out unprepared investors.

Rare events? Asymmetric payoffs? You might be asking, "what's that got to do with my investments?" As it turns out, it has a lot to do with how your financial life will unfold.

The frequency, or probability, of a result is not the main thing that matters when investing.

Rather it is the expected return (that is the probability times the payoff). This really matters when the results are skewed (or asymmetric). For example, having a 99% chance of winning is not a good bet if you only win $1 each time, but lose $1000 one percent of the time (an asymmetric payoff).

Your expected return would be a loss of $901. Note that although you'd expect to win 99% of the time, that one loss in a hundred (the rare event) would be more than enough to offset your winnings and then some.

In the financial realm you need to keep this in mind when investing in stocks. For symmetric results, expected returns are similar to the probability, but the stock market is not always symmetrical. In fact, it's usually not symmetrical.

The reason is that historical stock price data are really a sequence of events rather than a set of independent observations that many mathematical tools, such as statistics, require. But the causes of these events are hidden from us, recall our discussion on cause and effect in Chapter 6, thus making them appear to be random (or in statistical jargon, independent observations) when in fact they are not.

And because of this, even if it might look like it for long periods of time, the market does not follow a Normal (Gaussian) curve. Therefore the probabilities estimated by the Normal curve tend to underestimate the risks.

This means that tools built on a normal distribution, such as Modern Portfolio Theory (MPT) and pretty much most of the modern financial tools, also tend to underestimate the risks.

So why use such tools?

The reason is that they work well enough most of the time. There isn't anything better (much like democracy and capitalism, they're not anywhere near perfect but are currently the best political and economic systems available to us).

The caveat is to ensure that when a risk (that was underestimated) is realized, it won't hurt you (it is foreseen and protected against using methods and strategies that are outside the realm of standard statistical tools). But it all boils down to what you know.

If using MPT with index funds, for example, works efficiently in a large number of cases, then we take advantage of it. If in other cases it works, but not in the most efficient manner, then we accept there is no way to always obtain the most efficient result and move on.

If however it fails to work in a particular case, we ensure this case is taken into account so we will not suffer catastrophic damage. In essence we can use

MPT plus other techniques that will position us to do very well in the usual case, do fairly well in the unusual case and not be hurt in the rare case.

Unfortunately most investors don't do this.

Sometimes an investor will have a strategy that just happens to work well given a certain type of market (such as one that goes up).

This investor will look like a genius if this type of market occurs. However, we expect markets to change over time. Therefore if the investor doesn't have a plan to cover other market scenarios, he could be wiped out.

With millions of investors using many different investment systems, sheer luck will ensure that some of these investors' strategies mesh with the current market behaviour.

Similarly some investors will do well over long periods of time and in different market conditions just by chance.

If we have, say, 200 million people randomly picking a stock and then selling it after one week, some of them will pick a stock that goes up by 5% in that week. If we continue this for a year, we will have a small number who have successfully picked 52 stocks that went up by 5% each week.

These people would have made a lot of money. The press would be calling them financial geniuses and they'd be writing books and appearing on talk shows.

However the reality is they simply lucked out and used no skill whatsoever. Contrast this to someone you picked ahead of time to do the feat and then he did it; this would imply some sort of skill on that person's part.

One of the biggest mistakes today's investors make is focusing too much on results. Results are not the most important thing to look at.

Most people think that results are the key. If someone makes a killing in the stock market, people automatically assume that person is an investment genius or knows a secret nobody else does. That's not necessarily true. In fact it's not usually true.

What's more important is the way the results were achieved. The way you obtain a result is far more important than the actual result.

A lottery winner, for instance, who wins $25 million will have the same resources as a radiologist who built a net worth of $25 million through a long medical career.

The lottery winner can purchase the same kind of house in the same area, drive the same cars, attend the same shows and eat at the same fine restaurants.

However the lottery winner would most likely not be able to repeat that process if he tried a million more times. Whereas the radiologist most likely could.

For large life-changing sums such as that, it usually doesn't matter if the results are repeatable for that specific individual (although that's another story as various studies have shown lottery winners tend to spend their money and within a few years are back where they originally started).

However most people will not experience such a life-altering win. Most people see much smaller wins.

Taken down a few notches, we see similar results at the investment level.

Someone who picks a stock that explodes in price, through sheer luck, might consider himself an equal to somebody else who chose a stock, that also exploded in price, based on thorough research, logic and knowledge.

However in reality they are not equals. The latter person would have a high probability of repeating his performance while the former would have a high probability of losing all his money investing in stocks and hoping to get lucky.

That's why the process is so important and not just the results. And when it comes to the process you use, time has a way of quickly discarding the losers.

At this point you should have a healthy respect for risk and understand that diversification and allocation can help you minimize this risk.

As you've seen, you diversify based on low correlations between the stocks in your portfolio.

You've also seen there are two very effective ways (and one simplistic way) to allocate the amounts you invest in each equity that makes it into your portfolio.

However we've said nothing about how many equities your portfolio should contain. For the answer to that question we need look no further than the research of **Edwin J. Elton** and **Martin Gruber**.

Elton and Gruber studied this question and documented their findings in their book, "Modern Portfolio Theory and Investment Analysis."

They showed that 20 stocks with low correlations between them provided as much risk protection as a 500 or more stock portfolio. And going down to 8 low correlation stocks provided 81% of the risk protection.

So as a general rule of thumb, a properly diversified portfolio won't gain any additional risk protection by holding more than 20 equities.

Selecting 8 to 20 carefully chosen individual stocks should do the trick –
but you can get by with less when using certain kinds of index funds or sector
ETFs which are already somewhat diversified (and just so you know, Warren
Buffett has stated that you should hold no more than 10 high-quality,
fundamentally solid stocks in your portfolio. In fact he suggests holding 6 or
less – but Buffett notwithstanding, I'd still stick with a minimum of 8).

Before continuing let's pause to list some important things you should
consider.

1. Frequently look at a company's fundamentals (Balance Sheet, Income
   Statement and Cash Flows Statement) to ensure they stay at a place
   where you're still comfortable with them. If there's another company
   that has a high positive correlation with one you currently hold, but its
   fundamentals have now become better, then that's the company you
   should be in -- not the one you might currently be holding.
2. Portfolios can be sufficiently diversified over a few industries that
   have lower positive (or even negative) correlations between them. You
   don't need to buy a stock (or stocks) in *every* industry (in fact many of
   these industries are highly correlated anyways).
3. Invest in only the best companies after you've done your homework.
   Every day you should think, "if I had this amount of money in Cash
   (rather than stocks) and had to purchase stocks today, would I choose
   the ones I have now? Or would I choose another one?" If you
   answered "another one" then it might be time to upgrade your current
   holdings.
4. You should look at your entire financial situation when it comes to
   diversification. You shouldn't just look at your stocks in isolation. So
   if you own a house, a rental property, other assets and such, you're
   already diversifying over different asset classes and are lowering your
   risk. Therefore you can, possibly, afford to choose slightly riskier
   stocks. If all of your assets are in stocks, then you'd be prudent to
   choose good lower-risk ones. Furthermore as your equity portfolio
   grows significantly, you should pull out funds periodically and invest
   in other asset classes (such as rental properties and such).
5. Over-diversification is as bad as under-diversification. The reason
   most investors think they should have lots of stocks is because that's
   what the mutual fund companies do and say to do. Since most
   investors don't know how to diversify correctly, they simply buy into

that argument. But mutual fund companies have hundreds of millions to invest. So there is no way they can limit themselves to a handful of carefully selected stocks without affecting the market for those stocks. Furthermore, most funds have limits on the percentage of any single stock their fund can hold. Therefore they **have** to invest in lesser quality offerings in order to fulfill their mandate. They have no choice. However individual investors aren't restricted in this way because they cannot affect the market for widely traded stocks. Therefore they can invest in the cream of the crop.

6. Remember you're investing, not trading. Therefore 10% of your portfolio in one stock is okay. Following that logic you can be sufficiently diversified with 10 well chosen stocks.

7. If you own too many stocks and have to buy or sell a significant quantity to, say, rebalance or switch, trading costs can increase and the time required to manage your portfolio also increases.

Diversification and allocation are two of the most important factors in determining how your portfolio will perform and its specific risk characteristics.

However in order to maintain your allocations, you need to rebalance from time to time. Rebalancing is extremely important yet not many people do it – perhaps because they don't see the value, they don't know how or they just don't keep up with their investments.

The problem with any portfolio filled with stocks is the allocations change frequently because stock prices frequently change. For example, if we look at a portfolio with just two stocks, Stock A trading at $10 and Stock B at $20, and decide to invest an equal amount of money in each, then assuming we have $1,000 to invest, we will end up with 50 shares of Stock A and 25 shares of Stock B (that is, we will invest $500 in each stock).

Now fast forward a few months. Prices most likely won't remain at $10 and $20 respectively.

Let's say Stock A's price increases to $12 and Stock B falls to $15. At this point our portfolio would be worth $975 (25 shares of Stock B at $15 per share plus 50 shares of Stock A at $12 per share).

However Stock A would now comprise 61.5% of our portfolio while Stock B would only make up 38.5%. Quite a difference from our initial 50% allocation in each stock.

To fix this, we could simply rebalance back to our initial allocation. So we might decide to sell $108 of Stock A (that is, 9 shares) and use the proceeds to purchase 7 shares of stock B.

After this transaction, we would now own 41 shares of Stock A, down from 50 shares, trading at $12 per share ($492) and 32 shares of Stock B, up from 25 shares, trading at $15 per share ($480). We'd also have a small cash balance left over that we didn't use to purchase shares and we're ignoring transaction fees for this example.

The key point, however, is we have now adjusted our portfolio back to its target allocation of 50% each of Stock A and Stock B (actually 49.2% and 48% respectively, but that's close enough).

But why bother? Is there a good reason for doing this? As it turns out, there are several good reasons.

First and foremost it helps reduce risk. The reason to diversify over different stocks is to control risk. You don't want one stock disproportionately affecting your portfolio because if that stock crashes, your portfolio will crater along with it. By spreading your risk amongst multiple stocks, you insulate your portfolio from the behavior of just one stock.

So if one stock starts to overwhelm your portfolio because its performance has skyrocketed, you can keep it in check by rebalancing.

Another benefit is it automatically forces you to buy low and sell high. You'll sell a portion of a stock that has risen in value and use the proceeds to purchase shares in a stock that has either gone down or not moved up as much.

Most investors tend to do the opposite. They buy high, because of greed, and sell low, because of fear. Rebalancing eliminates this irrational behavior by automatically buying low and selling high without you having to make a conscious decision to do so. In effect, it removes your emotions from the investing equation.

And since well-performing stocks don't continually outperform and poor-performing stocks don't continually underperform, it makes sense to sell a portion of the outperformer in the expectation it will revert downward to its mean and use the proceeds to purchase the underperformer with the expectation it will revert upwards to its mean value.

Although not guaranteed, following this path can potentially increase your portfolio's overall returns.

So rebalancing can reduce risk and increase returns.

There's also an important side-benefit which I touched upon earlier. Rebalancing helps remove your emotions from the investing process. Since you're following a pre-planned strategy, you don't have to decide what to do. You simply take the appropriate action based on what occurs with stock prices in your portfolio.

Whether you're investing new money or simply working with existing funds, the decision of what to buy and sell is made for you. Without rebalancing, that decision is left to you and, if you're like the majority of investors, you'll likely buy more of what is going up and ignore (or even sell) stocks that are underperforming.

That's called chasing performance and it's probably the number one reason so many investors do poorly over the long term. Following a disciplined rebalancing strategy, however, helps you avoid this behavior and keeps you on a steady course to building wealth.

Hopefully I've convinced you that rebalancing is a good and necessary thing. The questions then become, "How often should I rebalance?" and "How should I do it?"

Right off the bat let me say there is no one way everyone agrees is best, but there are better ways and worse ways. So let's analyze some rebalancing methods and see where we end up.

It should be obvious that because stock prices change all the time, portfolios filled with stocks will usually be out of balance. However it doesn't make sense to constantly rebalance because buying and selling cost you time, having to constantly look at your portfolio, and money, in the form of transaction fees and taxes.

Because of this, the most common type of rebalancing is calendar rebalancing. You choose a time, say every 3 months, 6 months or annually, and rebalance at that point in time. The actual period doesn't matter much and although there's been loads of research done, nothing conclusive has been determined.

Perhaps for that reason, most investors choose to rebalance annually. It's usually beneficial to rebalance when you're about to add money to your portfolio, such as when you're contributing to a retirement account or investing your tax refund, so the annual date you choose should take this into account, but otherwise any date will do.

The benefit of calendar rebalancing is it's simple to do and simple to understand.

The downside is this type of rebalancing is very inefficient. Your portfolio will usually be out of balance most of the year and you won't be able to take consistent advantage of risk reduction, improved returns and buying low and selling high.

However calendar rebalancing is better than what most people do, which is not rebalancing at all.

A more effective rebalancing method is to use thresholds. The idea is to only rebalance when a stock drifts off target by a certain percentage, say an absolute 5% or a relative 25%.

For example, if one of your stock holdings has a target allocation of 20%, you would rebalance if its target allocation fell below 15% or rose above 25% (that is, an absolute 5%).

Or you could choose to rebalance using a relative 25%. So if your stock's allocation is, say, 10%, you would rebalance whenever the allocation rose above 12.5% or fell below 7.5% (because 2.5% is 25% of 10%).

Either method works but most people find using a relative number is better for smaller holdings (say when a stock comprises 15% or less of your portfolio) and an absolute number for larger holdings (above 15%).

The advantage of threshold rebalancing is, since it depends on price, you capture more rebalancing opportunities than with the simple calendar rebalancing method. On the other hand it's not so good if you hold lots of stocks in your portfolio because it has a tendency to rebalance based on small moves. However if you stick with selecting 10 or so well-chosen stocks, as I normally recommend, threshold rebalancing is a good way to go.

The disadvantage of this method is it takes more time. You have to constantly monitor your portfolio rather than simply look at it once a year. However with today's easily accessible software and spreadsheets, threshold rebalancing doesn't take as much time and effort as it did just a decade ago.

Another, less common, rebalancing method is to only rebalance when you're adding new money to your portfolio or making a withdrawal. In this instance you add money to the underperforming stocks or sell an over-performing stock to take money out. I personally don't think this is a good way to rebalance, but, again, it is better than doing nothing.

These three rebalancing methods are what most people who rebalance use; however the sad fact is most investors don't rebalance at all. So if you're doing any sort of rebalancing, you're light-years ahead of your investing colleagues.

So which method should you use? Which do I recommend? None of them.

If you're surprised by that answer, hang on a second because I'm about to describe what I believe to be a superior rebalancing method. It's called ***Opportunistic Rebalancing*** and has a number of advantages over all the methods I've just discussed.

Opportunistic Rebalancing has been shown, in a study by Gobind Daryanani, to not only control risk really well but to also provide better returns by capturing more buy low and sell high opportunities than other rebalancing methods.

The idea behind Opportunistic Rebalancing is to look frequently but only rebalance when it's profitable to do so. Traditional calendar rebalancing looks infrequently and rebalances each time it looks.

That's inefficient.

It's far better to constantly monitor what's happening in your portfolio and then decide whether it makes sense to rebalance.

Think of it this way. If you were standing some distance from a baseball pitcher and he threw a ball at you, would it make more sense to look where the ball is more frequently or less frequently before deciding whether you need to get out of the way or not?

It should be obvious that looking more frequently will give better results, in the case of the thrown ball, more frequent looking will result in you being hit less often.

Calendar rebalancing is like closing your eyes and only opening them once every, say, 20 seconds. However if the pitcher throws a ball an average of every 2 seconds, you end up missing 9 out of 10 opportunities to take evasive action.

Opportunistic Rebalancing is similar to keeping your eyes open most of the time. You can see when the pitcher throws the ball and follow the ball's trajectory. Then you can decide if you need to move in order to avoid being hit. You react based on the most current information rather than trying to guess when the ball will be thrown or where it currently is.

Opportunistic Rebalancing reacts to what stock prices do. It doesn't try to predict when to rebalance but only rebalances when prices move in such a way that it is profitable to do so.

The Daryanani study showed that an Opportunistic Rebalancing strategy more than doubled the calendar rebalancing benefits over a wide range of market conditions.

Why?

Well, it's been long known that although stocks sometimes experience short-term momentum, they will eventually revert to some mean value. In other words, when a stock's price is moving up, it tends to continue for a short time but then falls back to its mean value.

The opposite is also true much of the time. A stock's price will fall for a short time and then rise back to its mean value.

So stock prices tend to overshoot (or undershoot) their mean values before reverting. These price movements are actually short-term noise created when people overreact to good or bad news.

Therefore calendar rebalancing is at a disadvantage because it can't take advantage of this noise much of the time, while Opportunistic Rebalancing can.

So what exactly is Opportunistic Rebalancing?

It's a strategy similar to the relative threshold rebalancing strategy I described earlier, but it adds a new parameter called the tolerance band.

Like threshold rebalancing, if a stock is outside its threshold, it is rebalanced. Unlike threshold rebalancing, however, the stock is rebalanced to somewhere within the tolerance band, not to its initial allocation.

In addition, only stocks outside their respective tolerance bands are rebalanced. This means there's a higher probability not all stocks will need to be rebalanced, thus the number of trades required to complete the rebalancing is reduced.

In essence, the tolerance band provides some wiggle room for stock prices to move around without having to be rebalanced. It acts as a buffer that filters out unprofitable rebalancing activity.

Of course this begs the question of how to set the threshold and tolerance band. Daryanani's paper provides a comprehensive look at how he optimized and tested various settings, so I won't repeat everything here (if you're interested in learning how he arrived at his final results, you can search for his paper on Google, "*Opportunistic Rebalancing: A New Paradigm for Wealth Managers*").

Instead I'll simply give you his results.

According to Daryanani's research, Opportunistic Rebalancing works best over different kinds of market conditions when the threshold is set to 20% and the tolerance band is set to 50% of the threshold (so a 20% threshold will give a 10% tolerance band).

In addition, the interval (which is the number of times we look at the portfolio) should be set to biweekly, so we look at the portfolio once every two weeks but only rebalance if at least one stock's allocation is outside its threshold – in which case we rebalance by bringing ALL stocks whose allocations are outside their tolerance bands (note this is not their thresholds, but their tolerance bands) back to within their respective tolerance bands.

I'll clarify with an example. Suppose we have three stocks in our portfolio. Stock A makes up 50%, Stock B comprises 30% and Stock C's allocation is 20%.

So Stock A would have a threshold of 10% (20% of 50%) and a tolerance band of 5% (50% of the threshold). Similarly Stock B's threshold would be 6% with a tolerance of 3% and Stock C's threshold would be 4% with a tolerance of 2%.

To put this into concrete terms, we would rebalance if Stock A's allocation rose above 60% (that is, its initial allocation of 50% plus its threshold of 10%) or if its allocation fell below 40% (its initial allocation of 50% minus its threshold of 10%).

Similarly we would rebalance if Stock B's allocation rose above 36% or fell below 24% or if Stock C's allocation rose above 24% or fell below 16%.

Any of these would trigger a rebalancing event.

Now, once a rebalancing event has been triggered, we look at all stocks whose allocations are outside their associated TOLERANCE BANDS. Note a stock's allocation does not have to be outside its threshold to be rebalanced (of course one stock's allocation will be outside its threshold – that's how the rebalancing event was triggered in the first place), but the important point here is that other stocks whose allocations are outside their respective TOLERANCE BANDS will also be rebalanced.

Stocks whose allocations are within their tolerance bands will not be rebalanced.

Let's say Stock C's allocation rose to 27% (above the 24% threshold necessary to trigger a rebalancing event), Stock A's allocation rose to 54% (well within its threshold) and Stock B's allocation fell to 25% (again, within its threshold).

Because of Stock C, however, a rebalancing event is triggered.

So we now have to determine which stocks need to be rebalanced. To do this, we check to see if a particular stock's allocation is outside its tolerance band.

Stock A's tolerance band is from 45% to 55% (5% on either side of its initial allocation of 50%). Since Stock A's allocation only rose to 54%, it is within its tolerance band and therefore does not have to be rebalanced.

Stock B's tolerance band is from 27% to 33% (3% on either side of its initial allocation of 30%). However since Stock B's allocation fell to 25%, it is now outside its tolerance band (although it's still within its threshold) and therefore needs to be rebalanced.

And of course Stock C's allocation of 27% is now outside its tolerance band of 18% to 22% (and also above its threshold of 24%), so it too will have to be rebalanced.

Therefore we would rebalance Stock B to within its tolerance band of 27% to 33% and rebalance Stock C to within its tolerance band of 18% to 22%. Stock A would not be rebalanced.

Notice there is some wiggle room on how to rebalance Stock B and Stock C. We don't have to reset their allocations exactly to their initial allocations. So we have some flexibility to bring the allocations anywhere within their respective tolerance bands. This allows us to rebalance more efficiently. We could, say, rebalance Stock C by selling shares to bring its allocation to 18% and using the proceeds to purchase shares of Stock B so its allocation is now 33%. Or we could bring Stock C's allocation to 22% and Stock B's to 27%, or any other combination that works with the cash we generate from the sale of Stock C.

There's also one more thing you can do to wring out even more rebalancing benefits. By holding stocks that are uncorrelated, rebalancing takes advantage of the increased number of buy low and sell high opportunities and therefore potentially increases your portfolio's returns.

But let's go back to Daryanani's paper and summarize some of the benefits. He found that Opportunistic Rebalancing controls portfolio drift, significantly increases returns, reduces trading costs, reduces risk and provides better performance than simple calendar rebalancing.

Of course it takes more effort to implement an Opportunistic Rebalancing strategy than it does for other rebalancing strategies, however the benefits are well worth it.

I've built Opportunistic Rebalancing into the Pragmatic Investor software, so if you use this software, you automatically receive its benefits.

However you can implement the strategy for yourself with a spreadsheet or even a pencil and paper. Regardless of whether you choose to implement Opportunistic Rebalancing or not, it's a good idea to ensure you always use some sort of rebalancing strategy. And when you do, keep William Bernstein's advice in mind.

According to Bernstein, the benefit of rebalancing is contingent on 3 factors:

1. The volatility of the portfolio's assets. The more volatility, the better.
2. The correlations between assets in the portfolio. The lower the correlations, the higher the rebalancing returns.
3. The difference in returns among the assets. The lower the difference, the better. If asset returns are very different, it may be better not to rebalance at all.

And according to Portfolio Theory, when you diversify among uncorrelated stocks and rebalance, you reduce your risk and increase your returns. Remember, rebalancing is the key to maximizing your returns and lowering your risk. It's the closest thing to a free lunch you can expect from the stock market.

One final note. Investing needs are conceptually similar to Abraham Maslow's hierarchy of needs. Recall that in his paper, "A Theory of Human Motivation," Maslow defined five levels of needs. The lowest level, the Physiological level, included such things as breathing, food and water whereas the highest level, Self-Actualization, contained things like creativity and morality.

Maslow's thoughts were that in order to achieve the higher levels, the lower level needs must have first been fulfilled. In other words, before you can start looking at luxury-type things that aren't necessary to your survival, you must have your basic needs (such as food, clothing and shelter) satisfied. However it is the luxury-type things that greatly enhance your standard of living.

Similarly, when building your wealth, there is a portion of your investments you must have in order to retire with the basics. Then there's the part that will increase your standard of living.

It makes sense, then, to ensure the "must-have" part is extremely risk protected. Once that's done you can take varying degrees of risk with the other parts.

However taking risk does not mean speculating or gambling. Just as you wouldn't "throw away" all of your non-essential savings at a roulette wheel in

Vegas, you shouldn't "throw" it away chasing speculative stocks in hopes of getting rich quickly in a short period of time.

So go ahead and invest in higher risk stocks if you're comfortable doing so, but ensure you've done adequate research and your "must-have" investments are properly protected.

Before we leave the subject of diversification, I'll mention one more way to diversify that is not generally discussed. And that is diversifying by investment strategy. To best see why this is a good idea, we need only look at the superhero groups that were popular in the sixties (and are experiencing a resurgence in films today).

Remember the Fantastic Four, the Avengers, and the Justice League of America?

With members like the Human Torch, the Mighty Thor and Superman, they were always tromping across the planet (and sometimes across the galaxy) battling fiends with incredible powers. Somehow, however, they always found a way to defeat the villains and come back alive.

Time after time, facing unimaginable odds, the superhero teams of yesteryear conquered everything the bad guys threw at them. And not only conquered, but prevailed with wit, humor and outright aplomb.

So how did they do it? Yes, they had super powers, but so did the villains. Of course they were highly trained, but so too were the villains. And although they had right on their side, that didn't stop the villains from scheming and implementing plans that always seemed to have our heroes jumping from one predicament to another. Yet after everything was said and done, they always emerged victorious.

The trick was they were diversified. Take the Avenger Ant Man for example. He had the awesome power to shrink down to ant size while retaining the full strength of a human! Imagine that, the full strength of a human! Even your average run-of-the-mill super-villain had more strength in his little finger, but still Ant Man would inevitably contribute to that super-villain's demise.

Of course the Avengers also had the Mighty Thor. Now you'd think a guy able to hurl his hammer faster than the speed of light, smash mountains with one blow and call down lightning from the sky wouldn't need any help, but nonetheless he'd get in over his head quite often. And somebody like Ant Man, with all the strength of your average human, would come by and bail him out.

Super-villain scheme after super-villain scheme would inevitably fail because while some heroes could be neutralized, others would step up. Their diversified set of powers would inevitably win the day. So what lesson can we take away from these heroes and apply to the investment realm?

Well right off the bat we can see there's a huge benefit in diversification. If all the Avengers had the power of Thor, they'd be mighty powerful indeed (hence the moniker the MIGHTY Thor). However they'd also have been defeated long ago because the super villains would only have to come up with a way to neutralize Thor's power. It's the classic, "don't put all your super powers in one basket" approach. However the superhero team concept takes us one step further.

Not only shouldn't you put all of your super powers into one basket, but you should use different types of baskets.

Take Superman as another example. He had a diverse set of powers, including heat vision, super-speed, super-strength and x-ray vision. But he was also a member of the Justice League of America (JLA), which allowed him to not only use his diversified powers, but also gain the benefit of his teammates' powers. In effect the JLA ensured that not only were Superman's diversified powers put to good use, but the team benefited because all of its powers weren't in one basket (that is, Superman).

Translated to the investment side, this not only means you should definitely invest in a variety of asset classes (such as stocks, bonds, cash equivalent instruments and real estate), but you should also use a variety of investment strategies. Most investment advisors tell you to diversify your assets, but most (if not all) won't tell you to use a variety of strategies.

But, like the Avengers and the JLA, a diverse set of strategies (or heroes) can go a long way to achieving your goal. But only if you choose your strategies carefully.

Did you ever wonder why the super-villain teams inevitably failed? My guess is because they chose their teammates poorly. By their very nature super-villains were an untrustworthy lot. The fact they could rarely work together in harmony, like the heroes did, meant that they consistently failed at their objectives.

So a super-villain team, boasting the likes of the all-powerful Magneto, met defeat, again and again, by a super-hero team with the likes of Ant Man – with all the strength of your average human!

It should be clear, then, that the characteristics found in quality teammates were of prime importance. These characteristics were vastly more valuable than the actual powers a team member possessed. When the chips were down, you needed to completely trust your teammate's actions – even if you didn't know exactly what he was doing.

Similarly you need to choose your investment strategies carefully. Strategies that have proven themselves over and over and are completely trustworthy in all market conditions is the primary consideration. When the chips are down, you need complete confidence your strategies will see you through the rough times – even if you feel like throwing everything out and following your gut.

Let's face it, there are thousands of investment strategies out there and some do well given certain conditions. But which strategy would you rather follow? One that promises astronomical returns, but can turn on you at any second and completely wipe out your investments, or one that gets you where you want to go with much less risk?

I'm sure you already know the answer to that one.

So the next time you're thinking about diversifying, go one step further and think about diversifying your investment strategies as well as your assets.

ACTION PLAN

Ensure your portfolio is diversified correctly by selecting securities where the correlations between them are as low as possible. Next allocate these securities appropriately (using the Pragmatic Investor software's Asset Allocation function) and then rebalance as required – so you're always buying low and selling high.

*Once you've selected your stocks/funds and set up your initial allocations, monitor your investments and make minor course corrections when necessary. There are two types of course corrections: **Rebalancing** and **Replacing**.*

***Rebalancing**, as mentioned above, ensures you buy low and sell high. **Replacing** ensures that you're always holding the very best equities in your portfolio.*

Periodically run each of your stock investments through the Fundamental Analyzer and perform the necessary analysis again. If the results are still good then you need take no further action. However if the results have changed for the worse, it might be time to look at another stock to replace your current holding.

Ideally you want to replace your current holding with a stock that has a similar correlation value and is in a similar industry or sector – so as not to upset the allocation balance. However you can choose to select a stock in a completely different sector and/or with a different correlation – in which case you would rerun your allocation and then rebalance according to the new policy (i.e. results from the Asset Allocation function).

Doing this will ensure your portfolio is always at its most optimal and positioned to take advantage of future market moves even as you automatically buy low and sell high. This is very important. Ensure that you do it.

Chapter Fourteen

The Magical Cattle Ranch

(with apologies to Hans Christian Andersen)

A nd it came to pass that one day a group of dishonest wranglers arrived in the town of Genosha. They were cattlemen, they said, and knew how to raise the finest cattle that had ever set hoof on the Earth.

Not only were these cattle plump and healthy, but they were uncommonly large. One beast was enough to feed 30 families for weeks.

They said the cattle were of a magical variety and had the peculiar property of appearing leaner and smaller as a person's intelligence-level decreased. To the exceptionally dim-witted, these magical cattle appeared positively skeletal and scrawny.

"Those must be valuable cattle," thought the town's folk, and a small group of them paid the wranglers vast sums of money, in advance, to start a magical cattle ranch.

The wranglers set to work raising barns and erecting fences while bringing in hundreds of calves in covered boxcars in the dead of night. They told the townspeople that these calves were of the finest quality and contained the highest caliber magic they had ever seen in more than 20 years on the range.

The months rolled quickly on and the small group of investors waited patiently for any news. From time to time the wranglers released some information on their operation and it was always exceptionally good news, news such as, "the calves are growing faster than anticipated," or "we've spent less on food this month." However nobody was allowed to see the cattle.

The small group of investors started to become nervous. Anxious whispers could be heard about the town. But still the wranglers continued to say nothing but how well the ranch was operating.

Then one day the small group of investors received a substantial special dividend on their investment in the ranch. "A town in a far off land had wanted some of these magical cattle and had paid substantially for them," said the wranglers. "This is just a small portion of what is to come."

The investors were ecstatic and word quickly spread throughout the town. "I should like to invest in this ranch," said the Mayor as he heard the news. "I will send my Deputy Mayor to look at the ranch."

So the Deputy Mayor went to the ranch, where the wranglers were working, and looked around. But all he could see were malnourished, underfed and sickly cattle. But he did not say anything.

"Well, sir, how do you like our magical cattle?" said the wranglers. "Oh, they are the finest beasts I have ever seen," said the Deputy Mayor, not wanting to look stupid. "I will tell the Mayor he must invest straight away... why I'll invest myself."

"We are glad to hear that," said the wranglers. And so the cheats received even more money from the now-greedy townsfolk. And they went on working at the ranch. Everybody in town was talking about how large the magical cattle were and how they were going to use their investment returns to visit far off lands, build grand houses and hire gardeners, chefs and servants. And the wranglers continued to receive new investment funds.

Now the country's President was visiting and the Mayor, bursting with pride, took him to see the magical cattle ranch while relating the story of how the really stupid people perceived the cattle as small and scrawny but the most intelligent saw them as they were, large, rotund and extremely plump.

"What!" thought the Mayor when he arrived at the ranch and saw the scrawny cattle. "This is awful! Am I of such low intelligence? The voters cannot hear of this. What shall I say?"

"Oh, they are even larger than I had expected," said the Mayor aloud. And the President agreed while profusely shaking the wranglers' hands and gushing on about how beautiful the cattle were. The Mayor even proclaimed a special day and parade to celebrate the magical cattle ranch.

The people were drunk with glee and overjoyed as they prepared for the big parade and even wanted to rename the town's main street in honor of the wranglers.

The day finally arrived and the cattle were paraded down Genosha's main street. "What beautiful cattle," the people gushed, "and so large!" The doctors and lawyers and leading citizens all stood up and took turns complimenting the wranglers on the superb job they had done.

155

No one wanted to let it appear that he could see the cattle were small and underfed, for that would mean he had the lowest possible intelligence. The intelligence of a small child.

"BUT THE COWS ARE DYING!" said a little child.

After the dust had settled and the wranglers were found out and pressed, the head wrangler said that he would give back a total of $25 to all of the investors to make up for all that had gone wrong. And he urged the other wranglers to follow suit.

None of them did, however, as they were too busy visiting far off lands, building grand houses and hiring gardeners, chefs and servants. The head wrangler joined them a little later. And the wranglers lived happily ever after.

The END.

Chapter Fifteen

Taking Action

"Vision without action is a daydream. Action without vision is a nightmare."

Proverb

How does the saying go? "The road to hell is paved with good intentions." How about this one, "You can't wish your way into heaven." This is equally true of financial goals.

A goal is nothing more than a dream until you do something to make it a reality. The plain and simple truth is you can't wish your way to wealth. You've got to do something about it.

And remember, by choosing to do nothing you've made a choice, one that will eventually cost you large sums of money in lost profits.

Consider this, if your life continues in the same direction it's going now, where will you be one year from today? Will you be any closer to financial freedom? If you don't like the answer you get then do something to change it. For you to get different results in your life, you've got to do something different.

I mentioned the secret to amassing great wealth at the beginning of this book and I'll reiterate… **"The secret to obtaining great wealth is to make your money work hard for you, not to make you work hard for your money."** And that means you need to consistently build your investments. It really is that simple.

If you've read this far, you already know the major pitfalls investors face and the deadly investment mistakes they make. More importantly, however, you know how to avoid them and how to invest properly by correctly assessing a stock's fundamentals and then efficiently diversifying, allocating and rebalancing to lower your risk.

I've listed 7 of the deadliest investment mistakes, we talked about, below. Study them carefully. Memorize them. Avoid them successfully and you will do better than almost everyone else in the stock market. Your friends might even start asking for your expert advice.

THE 7 DEADLY INVESTMENT MISTAKES

1. Letting psychological biases and emotions rule your investment decisions.

2. Not having an investment objective.

3. Not having a plan.

4. Not spending your time wisely.

5. Trying to follow plans that are too difficult, time consuming or impossible.

6. Thinking you're going to get rich quickly in the stock market.

7. Not getting started right away.

You'll also find some interesting supplemental material in the appendices that contain valuable insights you can use to make your life better.

The concepts and tools described in this book will allow you to implement solid investment plans that can take you to your goals safely and efficiently.

Of course many people think to themselves, "that's great, but it sure looks like I have to do a lot of very tedious work – gathering the data and performing the various calculations." That's true. Analyzing company fundamentals and constructing efficient portfolios are time consuming tasks.

However there is an answer. The **Pragmatic Investor** software was designed to do all of the hard work for you – it automatically retrieves the relevant data from the Internet and performs the required calculations. All you have to do is enter ticker symbols and click a few mouse buttons. No searching for company financial data and no calculator required.

It helps you find stocks with good fundamentals and then it lets you efficiently diversify and allocate your portfolio. After that, sit back and monitor your investments every so often with the software's powerful functions, making changes and rebalancing when necessary.

If you're doing that, you're on your way to building solid wealth in the stock market.

So don't worry, go out and spend your time pursuing activities you enjoy. Your investments will take care of themselves and then they will eventually take care of you!

The Magic Story

I first read the "Magic Story" a few years ago and found it quite interesting. So here it is reprinted in all its glory.

The Magic Story
by Frederick Von Renesselaer Day

I nasmuch as I have evolved from my experience the one great secret of success for all worldly undertakings, I deem it wise, now that the number of my days is nearly counted, to give to the generations that are to follow me the benefit of whatsoever knowledge I possess.

I do not apologize for the manner of my expression, nor for the lack of literary merit, the latter being, I think, its own apology. Tools much heavier than the pen have been my portion, and moreover, the weight of years has somewhat palsied the hand and brain; nevertheless, the fact I can tell, and what I deem the meat within the nut.

What matters it, in what manner the shell be broken, so that the meat be obtained and rendered useful? I doubt not that I shall use, in the telling, expressions that have clung to my memory since childhood; for, when men attain the number of my years, happenings of youth are like to be clearer to their perceptions than are events of recent date; nor doth it matter much how a thought is expressed, if it be wholesome and helpful, and finds the understanding.

Much have I wearied my brain anent the question, how best to describe this recipe for success that I have discovered, and it seems advisable to give it as it came to me; that is, if I relate somewhat of the story of my life, the directions for agglomerating the substances, and supplying the seasoning for the accomplishment of the dish, will plainly be perceived. Happen they may; and that men may be born generations after I am dust, who will live to bless me for the words I write.

My father, then, was a seafaring man who, early in life, forsook his vocation, and settled on a plantation in the colony of Virginia, where, some years thereafter, I was born, which event took place in the year 1642; and that was over a hundred years ago. Better for my father had it been, had he hearkened to the wise advice of my mother, that he remain in the calling of his education; but he would not have it so, and the good vessel he captained was bartered for the land I spoke of.

Here begins the first lesson to be acquired:

> *Man should not be blinded to whatsoever merit exists in the opportunity which he hath in hand, remembering that a thousand promises for the future should weigh as naught against the possession of a single piece of silver.*

When I had achieved ten years, my mother's soul took flight, and two years thereafter my worthy father followed her. I, being their only begotten, was left alone; howbeit, there were friends who, for a time, cared for me; that is to say, they offered me a home beneath their roof – a thing which I took advantage of for the space of five months. From my father's estate there came to me naught; but, in the wisdom that came with increasing years, I convinced myself that his friend, under whose roof I lingered for some time, had defrauded him, and therefore me.

Of the time from the age of twelve and a half until I was three and twenty, I will make no recital here, since that time hath naught to do with this tale; but some time after, having in my possession the sum of sixteen guineas, ten, which I had saved from the fruits of my labor, I took ship to Boston town, where I began to work first as a cooper, and thereafter as a ship's carpenter, although always after the craft was docked; for the sea was not amongst my desires.

Fortune will sometimes smile upon an intended victim because of pure perversity of temper. Such was one of my experiences. I prospered, and at seven and twenty, owned the yard wherein, less than four years earlier, I had worked for hire. Fortune, howbeit, is a jade who must be coerced; she will not be coddled. Here begins the second lesson to be acquired:

> *Failure exists only in the grave. Man, being alive, hath not yet failed; always he may turn about and ascend by the same path he descended by; and there may be one that is less abrupt (albeit longer of achievement), and more adaptable to his condition.*

About this time, Disaster (which is one of the heralds of broken spirits and lost resolve), paid me a visit. Fire ravaged my yards, leaving me nothing in its blackened paths but debts, which I had not the coin wherewith to defray.

I labored with my acquaintances, seeking assistance for a new start, but the fire that had burned my competence, seemed also to have consumed their sympathies. So it happened, within a short time, that not only had I lost all, but I was hopelessly indebted to others; and for that they cast me into prison.

It is possible that I might have rallied from my losses but for this last indignity, which broke down my spirits so that I became utterly despondent.

Upward of a year I was detained within the jail; and, when I did come forth, it was not the same hopeful, happy man, content with his lot, and with confidence in the world and its people, who had entered there.

Life has many pathways, and of them by far the greater number lead downward. Some are precipitous, others are less abrupt; but ultimately, no matter at what inclination the angle may be fixed, they arrive at the same destination – failure. And here begins the third lesson:

> *Fortune is ever elusive, and can only be retained by force. Deal with her tenderly and she will forsake you for a stronger man. (In that, me-thinks, she is not unlike other women of my knowledge.)*

When I came forth from prison, I was penniless. In all the world I possessed naught beyond the poor garments which covered me, and a walking stick which the turnkey had permitted me to retain, since it was worthless.

Being a skilled workman, howbeit, I speedily found employment at good wages; but, having eaten of the fruit of worldly advantage, dissatisfaction possessed me. I became morose and sullen; whereat, to cheer my spirits, and for the sake of forgetting the losses I had sustained, I passed my evenings at the tavern.

Not that I drank overmuch of liquor, except on occasion (for I have ever been somewhat abstemious), but that I could laugh and sing, and parry wit and *badinage* with my ne'er-do-well companions; and here might be included the fourth lesson:

> *Seek comrades among the industrious, for those who are idle will sap your energies from you.*

It was my pleasure at that time to relate, upon slight provocation, the tale of my disasters, and to rail against the men whom I deemed to have wronged me, because they had seen fit not to come to my aid.

Moreover, I found childish delight in filching from my employer, each day, a few moments of the time for which he paid me. Such a thing is less honest than downright theft. This habit continued and grew upon me until the day dawned which found me not only without employment, but also without character, which meant that I could not hope to find work with any other employer in Boston town.

It was then that I regarded myself a failure. I can liken my condition at that time for naught more similar than that of a man who, descending the steep side of a mountain, loses his foothold. The farther he slides, the faster he goes.

I have also heard this condition described by the word Ishmaelite, which I understand to be a man whose hand is against everybody, and who thinks that the hands of every other man are against him; and here begins the fifth lesson:

> *The Ishmaelite and the leper are the same, since both are abominations in the sight of man –*
> *albeit they differ much, in that the former may be restored to perfect health. The former is entirely the result of imagination; the latter has poison in his blood.*

I will not discourse at length upon the gradual degeneration of my energies. It is not good ever to dwell much upon misfortunes (which saying is also worthy of remembrance). It is enough if I add that the day came where I possessed naught wherewith to purchase food and raiment, and I found myself like unto a pauper, save at infrequent times when I could earn a few pence, or mayhap, a shilling.

Steady employment I could not secure, so I became emaciated in body, and naught but skeleton in spirit.

My condition, then, was deplorable; not so much for the body, be it said, as for the mental part of me, which was sick unto death. In my imagination I deemed myself ostracized by the whole world, for I had sunk very low indeed; and here begins the sixth and final lesson to be acquired, (which cannot be told in one sentence, nor in one paragraph, but must needs be adopted from the remainder of this tale).

Well do I remember my awakening, for it came in the night, when, in truth, I did awake from sleep. My bed was a pile of shavings in the rear of the cooper shop where once I had worked for hire; my roof was the pyramid of casks, underneath which I had established myself.

The night was cold, and I was chilled, albeit, paradoxically, I had been dreaming of light and warmth and of the depletion of good things.

You will say, when I relate the effect the vision had on me, that my mind was affected. So be it, for it is the hope that the minds of others might be likewise influenced which disposes me to undertake the labor of this writing.

It was the dream which converted me to the belief – nay, to the knowledge – that I was possessed of two entities: and it was my own better self that afforded me the assistance for which I had pleaded in vain from my acquaintances. I have heard this condition described by the word "double." Nevertheless, that word does not comprehend my meaning. A double, can be naught more than a double, neither half being possessed of individuality. But I will not philosophize, since philosophy is naught but a suit of garments for the decoration of a dummy figure.

Moreover, it was not the dream itself which affected me; it was the impression made by it, and the influence that it exerted over me, which accomplished my enfranchisement. In a word, then, I encouraged my other identity. After toiling through a tempest of snow and wind, I peered into a window and saw that other being. He was rosy with health; before him, on the hearth, blazed a fire of logs; there was a conscious power and force in his demeanor; he was physically and mentally muscular. I rapped timidly upon the door, and he bade me enter. There was a not unkindly smile of derision in his eyes as he motioned me to a chair by the fire; but he uttered no word of welcome; and, when I had warmed myself, I went forth again into the tempest, burdened with the shame which the contrast between us had forced upon me. It was then that I awoke; and here cometh the strange part of my tale, for, when I did awake, I was not alone. There was a Presence with me; intangible to others, I discovered later, but real to me.

The Presence was in my likeness, yet it was strikingly unlike. The brow, not more lofty than my own, yet seemed more round and full; the eyes, clear, direct, and filled with purpose, glowed with enthusiasm and resolution; the lips, chin – ay, the whole contour of face and figure was dominant and determined.

He was calm, steadfast, and self-reliant; I was cowering, filled with nervous trembling, and fearsome of intangible shadows. When the Presence turned away, I followed, and throughout the day I never lost sight of it, save when it disappeared for a time beyond some doorway where I dared not enter; at such places, I awaited its return with trepidation and awe, for I could not help wondering at the temerity of the Presence (so like myself, and yet so unlike), in daring to enter where my own feet feared to tread.

It seemed also as if purposely, I was led to the place and to the men where, and before whom I most dreaded to appear; to offices where once I had transacted business; to men with whom I had financial dealings. Throughout the day I pursued the Presence, and at evening saw it disappear beyond the portals of a hostelry famous for its cheer and good living. I sought the pyramid of casks and shavings.

Not again in my dreams that night did I encounter the Better Self (for that is what I have named it), albeit, when, perchance, I awakened from slumber, it was near to me, ever wearing that calm smile of kindly derision which could not be mistaken for pity, nor for condolence in any form. The contempt of it stung me sorely.

The second day was not unlike the first, being a repetition of its forerunner, and I was again doomed to wait outside during the visits which the Presence paid to places where I fain would have gone had I possessed the requisite courage. It is fear which deporteth a man's soul from his body and rendereth it a thing to be despised. Many a time I essayed to address it but enunciation rattled in my throat, unintelligible; and the day closed like its predecessor.

This happened many days, one following another, until I ceased to count them; albeit, I discovered that constant association with the Presence was producing an effect on me; and one night when I awoke among the casks and discerned that he was present, I made bold to speak, albeit with marked timidity.

"Who are you?" I ventured to ask; and I was startled into an upright posture by the sound of my own voice; and the question seemed to give pleasure to my companion, so that I fancied there was less of derision in his smile when he responded.

"I am that I am," was the reply. "I am he who you have been; I am he who you may be again; wherefore do you hesitate? I am he who you were, and whom you have cast out for other company. I am the man made in the image of God, who once possessed your body. Once we dwelt within it together, not in harmony, for that can never be, nor yet in unity, for that is impossible, but as tenants in common who rarely fought for full possession. Then, you were a puny thing, but you became selfish and exacting until I could no longer abide with you, therefore I stepped out. There is a plus-entity and minus-entity in every human body that is born into the world.

Whichever one of these is favored by the flesh becomes dominant; then is the other inclined to abandon its habitation, temporarily or for all time. I am the plus-entity of yourself; you are the minus-entity. I own all things; you possess naught. That body which we both inhabited is mine, but it is unclean, and I will not dwell within it. Cleanse it, and I will take possession."

"Why do you pursue me?" I next asked of the Presence.

"You have pursued me, not I you. You can exist without me for a time, but your path leads downward, and the end is death. Now that you approach the end, you debate if it be not politic that you should cleanse your house and invite me to enter. Step aside, from the brain and the will; cleanse them of your presence; only on that condition will I ever occupy them again."

"The brain has lost its power," I faltered. "The will is a weak thing, now; can you repair them?"

"*Listen!*" said the Presence, and he towered over me while I cowered abjectly at his feet. "To the plus-entity of a man, all things are possible. The world belongs to him – is his estate. He fears naught, dreads naught, stops at naught; he asks no privileges, but demands them; he dominates, and cannot cringe; his requests are orders; opposition flees at his approach; he levels mountains, fills in vales, and travels on an even plane where stumbling is unknown."

166

Thereafter, I slept again, and, when I awoke, I seemed to be in a different world. The sun was shining and I was conscious that birds twittered above my head. My body, yesterday trembling and uncertain, had become vigorous and filled with energy. I gazed upon the pyramid of casks in amazement that I had so long made use of it for an abiding place, and I was wonderingly conscious that I had passed my last night beneath its shelter.

The events of the night recurred to me, and I looked about me for the Presence. It was not visible, but anon I discovered, cowering in a far corner of my resting place, a puny abject shuddering figure, distorted of visage, deformed of shape, disheveled and unkempt of appearance. It tottered as it walked, for it approached me piteously; but I laughed aloud, mercilessly. Perchance I knew then that it was the minus-entity, and that the plus-entity was within me; albeit I did not then realize it. Moreover, I was in haste to get away; I had no time for philosophy. There was much for me to do – much; strange it was that I had not thought of that yesterday. But yesterday was gone – today was with me – it had just begun.

As had once been my daily habit, I turned my steps in the direction of the tavern, where formerly I had partaken of my meals. I nodded cheerily as I entered, and smiled in recognition of returned salutations. Men who had ignored me for months bowed graciously when I passed them on the thoroughfare. I went to the washroom, and from there to the breakfast table; afterwards, when I passed the taproom, I paused a moment and said to the landlord:

"I will occupy the same room that I formerly used, if perchance, you have it at disposal. If not, another will do as well, until I can obtain it."

Then I went out and hurried with all haste to the cooperage. There was a huge wain in the yard, and men were loading it with casks for shipment. I asked no questions, but, seizing barrels, began hurling them to the men who worked atop of the load. When this was finished, I entered the shop. There was a vacant bench; I recognized its disuse by the litter on its top.

It was the same at which I had once worked. Stripping off my coat, I soon cleared it of impedimenta. In a moment more I was seated, with my foot on the vice-lever, shaving staves.

It was an hour later when the master workman entered the room, and he paused in surprise at sight of me; already there was a goodly pile of neatly shaven staves beside me, for in those days I was an excellent workman; there was none better, but, alas! now, age hath deprived me of my skill. I replied to his unasked question with the brief, but comprehensive sentence: "I have returned to work, sir." He nodded his head and passed on, viewing the work of other men, albeit anon he glanced askance in my direction.

Here endeth the sixth and last lesson to be acquired, although there is more to be said, since from that moment I was a successful man, and ere long possessed another shipyard, and had acquired a full competence of worldly goods.

I pray you who read, heed well the following admonitions, since upon them depend the word "success" and all that it implies:

> *Whatsoever you desire of good is yours. You have but to stretch forth your hand and take it.*

Learn that the consciousness of dominant power within you is the possession of all things attainable.

Have no fear of any sort or shape, for fear is an adjunct of the minus-entity.

If you have skill, apply it; the world must profit by it, and therefore, you.

Make a daily and nightly companion of your plus-entity; if you heed its advice, you cannot go wrong.

Remember, philosophy is an argument; the world, which is your property, is an accumulation of facts.

Go therefore, and do that which is within you to do; take no heed of gestures which would beckon you aside; *ask of no man's permission to perform.*

The minus-entity requests favors; the plus-entity grants them. Fortune waits upon every footstep you take; seize her, bind her, hold her, for she is yours; she belongs to you.

Start out now, with these admonitions in your mind.

Stretch out your hand, and grasp the plus, which, maybe, you have never made use of, save in great emergencies. Life is an emergency most grave.

Your plus-entity is beside you now; cleanse your brain, and strengthen your will. It will take possession. It waits upon you.

Start tonight; start now upon this new journey.

Be always on your guard. Whichever entity controls you, the other hovers at your side; beware lest the evil enter, even for a moment.

My task is done. I have written the recipe for "success." If followed, it cannot fail. Wherein I may not be entirely comprehended, the plus-entity of whosoever reads will supply the deficiency; and upon that Better Self of mine,

I place the burden of imparting to generations that are to come, the secret of this all-pervading good – the secret of being what you have it within you to be.

An Essay on Investing

The best definition I can give on investing is, that it is the mechanism available to everyone by which they can transfer wealth earned today to tomorrow, and not only transfer but multiply and increase, through compounding, so that their future lives can be transformed into something exciting and worry-free, enriched with abundant time to allow them to live as they desire without the constraints and burdens imposed by a lack of finances so often foisted upon the majority.

Investing is a gateway to freedom and prosperity. It is a tool that when properly used brings wealth and its attendant benefits but when improperly used is the saddest and most misunderstood joke played upon unsuspecting mankind.

Saddest because it creates the illusion that wealth is just around the corner, implies the carrot is right there for the taking, promises vast rewards and riches easily attained, yet in the end, after making investors jump through myriad hoops and time wasting activities, fails miserably to deliver.

Misunderstood because its inherent simplicity, that is to buy low and sell high, is oft times equated with ease, but simplicity and ease are two very different animals – the latter being like riding a well trained horse, where horse and rider behave as one, everything fits and destinations come and go by easily. The former is like an unbroken bronco, calm from afar giving the illusion of ridability, but nevertheless underestimated, ferocious and not easily tamed.

The fact that many assume, without much thought, that simplicity is identical to ease, then make decisions and go forth with actions based upon that assumption, shows that they know little about investing, and have even less discipline because they will not take the smallest stitch in time to contemplate the way things truly are.

Simple things, by their very nature, appear easy perhaps due to their transparency, inherent logical construction, intuitive nature or the ease at which their concepts can be grasped and understood, but not all simple things are easy as anyone who has tried to lose weight using the simplest of all methods, that being exercise and proper nutrition, can attest.

Some of the simplest things are the most difficult for humans to attain. Investing is one such beast. Again it relates to discipline. Human emotion is forever the enemy of the investor and emotion must always be controlled by sheer force of will, determination and perseverance which when combined gives rise to discipline.

Without discipline the game is over even before it begins. The result is preordained and while the moves have yet to be played, they matter not one bit in the end for the outcome has already been determined – destined to fail in a void of ill-conceived, haphazard actions lacking not just a goal but a good plan as well.

But discipline alone is not enough. Discipline must be built atop the solid foundation of knowledge. Even the most disciplined of travelers following the wrong path will end up tired, hungry and lost.

In that respect there can be no "or" condition. It cannot be knowledge "or" discipline, no independent, separated concepts, rather success must come from both together, from a melding of discrete entities, from a marriage of equals, from the synergies created by the union where the whole is most definitely much greater than the sum of the parts.

Hence the mind must be understood and controlled, its natural tendencies, its entrenched habits, diverted if not permanently changed; and this can only be achieved through constant vigilance and introspection. The mind cannot be allowed to roam free in its natural domain doing whatever it wants at any particular moment in time. Without a tight rein it will lead to places best left unvisited.

As such, considerable effort should be devoted to such a pursuit, but as we well know, this is no trivial task, to rein in the mind, it is no cakewalk or romp in the park; there is no royal road to riches.

If it were not so, every investor would be a millionaire many times over. But as the facts bear out, the vast majority of investors are not rich, they're not wealthy nor are they even almost rich. Rather they have trouble keeping up with even the simplest of investment mechanisms – the index fund.

The reason is the aforementioned lack of discipline and knowledge. Human nature is such that it craves action, it loves a good chase and gets bored very quickly waiting or doing nothing or sitting on its hands. Yet, for investing success, the overwhelming evidence suggests just the opposite; investors, once set up correctly, should wait, do nothing, sit on their hands, albeit making minor course corrections along the way, and refrain from chasing the latest hot stocks. The mind, however, has other plans and the investment industry is all too willing to accommodate it as long as there is money to be made.

Any excuse to sell an idea, whether it is a good idea or not, is floated to the unsuspecting public – so long as it will make truckloads of money; and the more short-term action, the more buzz that can be generated in the media, the more adrenalin fuelling, ticker watching, immediately gratifying the idea the better it will be because the more money it will make for the investment houses selling it.

The fact the average investor will be worse off than if he simply bought a good index fund and held it is not so much blatantly hidden as it is pushed to the side, underemphasized and overwhelmed by the billion dollar marketing schemes that permeate the current investment climate.

Play to human nature and you can't help but make money, appears to be the marketing mantra.

Unfortunately most investors will fall for this siren song because they won't have the knowledge or discipline to resist, they won't have control over their minds, they won't put a plan in place to remove emotions from the investment equation and more than likely they will succumb to the intoxicating game of short-term action and instant gratification touted by the investment community. As a result billions of dollars will flow from individual investors' pockets directly into the investment firms' just as surely as money inevitably finds its way from a gambler's account into the casino's.

If indeed that was the only possibility, then it would no doubt be better to save considerable effort and throw up your hands in surrender, put your money under the mattress and hope, in vain, for a government sponsored retirement plan to bail you out.

But just as not all sheep follow the flock, as David the Shepard saw firsthand on more than one occasion, so it is that you don't have to follow the crowd, you can find your own way, another way, a better way and use a well thought out plan that when properly conceived and fully implemented will make you rich beyond your wildest expectations.

The solution is not only simple, but easy as well.

Remove short-term investment decisions from your emotions' control and you will be far better off down the road. Put all your efforts into setting appropriate goals and finding good plans to help you achieve them – all the while ignoring the rhetoric and noise that will inevitably appear as it always has in the past.

Your future self will look back and thank you for the wise decision you made today. Your friend's future self, watching his pennies and delivering morning newspapers to make ends meet, will look back longingly and no doubt begrudgingly at his past self and wonder how he could have fallen for the schemes and manipulations that passed for investment advice in 2008; too late will he have realized the wisdom in the words of Warren Buffett who said, "the market, like the Lord, helps those who help themselves. But unlike the Lord, the market does not forgive those who know not what they do."

Appendix Three

Software

I n the past decade, the Internet has opened the investment world to millions of people like never before. Unfortunately it has also complicated the subject by introducing reams of advice that not only contradict, but too often is just plain wrong.

This book gives you the inside scoop on how to **really** invest successfully in the stock market. There are many ways of investing and they range from worthless to excellent. The Pragmatic Investor distills the research and strategies created by some of the smartest investment researchers and practitioners into an easily understandable strategy that you can use to invest better than the vast majority of people.

Knowing how to invest properly can be both fun and profitable. As you've seen, there are simple changes you can make that allow you to increase your returns, minimize your risk and do more with your investments.

We developed the companion software to help you automatically implement the concepts and ideas you've read about in the book. It automates almost everything so that you receive all of the benefits in a fraction of the time it would normally take – typically just a few hours a month.

You see, the concepts you've just read about are not difficult to understand, but implementing them can be tedious and time-consuming. Fundamental analysis, for example, requires numerous calculations and even the most conscientious of us will make mistakes.

Furthermore, asset allocation requires even more complex calculations that aren't feasible to perform on a calculator. That's where the computer comes in.

Using your computer and the **Pragmatic Investor** software, you can easily automate the tedious pieces.

You'll quickly use the best, proven stock selection, diversification, asset allocation and rebalancing strategies to your advantage and, as a bonus, you'll be able to subscribe to hundreds of free News feeds, categorize them to your tastes and read only the News in which you're interested – right online with the built-in News Reader.

You'll also find that it's easy to use and has a very low learning curve. In fact, most investors start using it in less than five minutes after installation.

This powerful software can save you hundreds of hours each year and free you from the error-prone and tedious tasks required to safely boost your investment profits.

To get the market-beating advantage of the new Pragmatic Investor software or to learn more, please visit **PragmaticInvestor.com**

About the Author

Mark Hing is President of Aptus Communications Inc., a software and consulting company that specializes in bringing proven investment strategies and methods to individual investors.

Since 1999, Aptus has been selling easy-to-use investment software designed to make investing more profitable, less risky and more rewarding.

By combining tested algorithms with crystal clear user interfaces and leveraging the Internet's ability to deliver accurate financial data, Mark's software has allowed thousands of people to invest successfully for themselves.

He has also published numerous articles, taught at colleges and large corporations, presented papers at a variety of technical conferences and been the editor of a monthly technology magazine.

The Pragmatic Investor is his first book.

Mark lives in the seaside town of Qualicum Beach, British Columbia with his wife, children and their two cats.

www.ingramcontent.com/pod-product-compliance
Lightning Source LLC
Chambersburg PA
CBHW031934190326
41519CB00007B/529